To Italy, With Love

a memoir

by

Kate Krenz

with notes and an Epilogue

by Kim Krenz

Krenz, Kate
To Italy, With Love : a memoir / by Kate Krenz.

Originally published 1987 under the title: Our love affair with Italy.
ISBN 0-9681749-1-4

1. Krenz, Kate – Travel – Italy.   2. Italy – Description and travel.
I. Krenz, Kate. Our love affair with Italy.   II. Title.

DG430.K74 2006   914.504'926   C2006-905825-3

Front Cover Design by RGB Imaging Ltd., Lakefield Ontario. Concept by Kim Krenz.

Published by 4th Floor Press, Inc.
First Printing 2006
www.4thfloorpress.com

To Italy, With Love

INTRODUCTION

Love has provided the inspiration for this book, Kate's love of Italy and the Italians, our love for each other, and my love for her now that she is gone. Whatever shortcomings the book may have, they do not stem from a lack of honest sentiment.

It is hard for me to think of Kate in the past tense after over sixty-four years of marriage. Our long life together has led us through many interesting adventures and episodes in Canada, Scotland, Italy and in other countries. The Italian experience has produced a charming book by Kate, "Our Love Affair With Italy," about our stay in Italy between 1962 and 1964, written in long-hand almost entirely from memory, with a few additions from notes and from letters sent home to Canada. The book was transcribed from Kate's script to digital text by a free-lance secretary in Barbados during our stay there for a CIDA project. A run of a thousand copies was printed privately in Peterborough, Ontario, by Maxwell Press in 1987. The book has been well received by all who have read it. Andrea Negrotto-Cambiaso, a former Italian ambassador to Canada, loved it and said the book was a true statement of Italian character. There are only a handful of copies left.

Kate died on 15 January 2005, four days after her ninety-second birthday, and it was a great joy to her to receive an enthusiastic response from a reader of her book shortly before she died. In the months after her death, I became convinced that an effort should be made to give her work wider exposure. I knew that the work would require editing and reorganization before it could be given to a publishing firm. I resolved to undertake the task, not of rewriting Kate's story, which should remain inviolate, but of editing it and, where necessary, rearranging the text and supporting it with introductory or explanatory material. To this end, I have recently made a three weeks stay in the region of Italy where we lived, during which I renewed friendships, revisited locations, absorbed local atmosphere and brought Kate's observations up to date. I have tried to make my contributions inconspicuous. I cannot match Kate's writing, and can do no more than provide a new frame for her *capolavoro*.

Reliving the experiences of our times together in Italy has been very difficult for me, for I have so often heard Kate's voice in the words she has written. This will not, of course, affect the general reader, to whom Kate will be no more than a name attached to a few photographs. Perhaps, though, after an exposure to the spirit that shines through her writing, the general reader, too, will come to an appreciation of the person that she was, and why Italy welcomed her with open arms.

In this book, I have been erecting a monument to Kate, using her own words. This Introduction would not be complete without my acknowledging the help and support I have had from 4th Floor Press in producing the book. Anne Bougie, Vice-President, Production, has been a constant companion and advisor during the production. Johanna M. Bates, President, has maintained a firm, guiding hand throughout. My thanks are due to both.

Kim Krenz
Lakefield, June 2006

Chapter 1

We Travel to Italy

The events leading up to our sojourn in Italy are simple to relate. In 1961, we were living in a winterized cottage on the majestic Ottawa River near Deep River. I was working as a research scientist at the Chalk River Nuclear Laboratories of Atomic Energy of Canada. We had recently been in Edinburgh where I had had a fellowship in the Department of Natural Philosophy (Physics). On returning to Canada I had been assigned to work in a different field, and though things went well at first, in time it became painfully obvious that I was ill equipped to perform the duties the position demanded. As a gesture of recognition of earlier achievements and an evident desire to extract me from a situation no longer supportable, I was appointed Canadian Liaison Scientist to Euratom, the atomic energy agency of the European Common Market. I had the choice of working from a base in Belgium or a base in Italy.

We had often visited Italy while we were in Edinburgh, for my aunt, Dorothy St. Clair, was stationed at the American

Consulate in Genoa. She boarded in Genoa with Signora Giuseppina Beltrami, known as "Pina," one of the most voluble and energetic women that Kate and I had ever met. A two weeks stay in Brussels convinced me that the Italian post was infinitely preferable. Kate would have approached either posting with characteristic energy and enthusiasm, but was happy to be moving to Italy.

August 24, 1961 was a great day in our lives and I remember it vividly. I was alone all day, a rare occurrence for me in summer. Unfortunately we have no children, so nephews and nieces and great ones are especially dear to us, and some were usually with us in summer. Kim's mother who, since her retirement from the U.S. Consular Service, had lived with us, was away visiting one of her daughters. Not only was I alone all day, but not even the phone had rung. Suddenly, earlier than the normal home coming time, there was our car easing its way over the rocky road. My instant thought was that Kim must be ill and I ran to see. His eyes were not shining with excitement; they were fairly blazing, and I knew something special must be afoot.When he suggested a scotch out under the pine trees, I knew it for certain. After twenty-one years of marriage, he knew that on a summer afternoon my drink is iced tea. So when he had the chairs arranged for the best view of the river, I was sipping my scotch and waiting for the momentous news.

"Atomic Energy is going to send a liaison scientist to "Euratom," he began.

"What is Euratom?"

"It is the work on atomic energy being carried on by the six countries in the European Common Market. The main labs are in Northern Italy."

"Yes, yes, go on, go on."

"Well, at work today they told me that due to my attitude toward people and my ability with languages, that I am the person to go."

"Oh, how wonderful, how wonderful !"

Just how wonderful it would be we could imagine. We sat on under our pine trees lost in the wonder of two whole years in Italy. I remember thinking that I was at a time in life for stock-taking and what an opportunity to be able to take stock over there. On that summer day we got into our bathing suits in a dreamlike state, went swimming, sat on our favourite rock and went on dreaming and planning. We had plenty of time to dream and plan for we did not leave Canada until April.

I share Kim's attitude towards people, which means we just naturally like people. Unfortunately, I do not share his ability with languages. He grew up in China speaking both Chinese and English and this, plus his good ear for sound, means that languages come easily to him. With me, it is a fight all the way. I started fighting as soon as I knew we were to go, for I was determined to get the most from our two years in "La Bella Italia." I pinned up vocabularies over the kitchen sink and the laundry tubs, and I propped them up in the bathroom and the bedroom. I kept doggedly at them; but I was not too concerned with my slowness, for the memory of the great kindness and courtesy we had found in Italy was very reassuring. What really did concern me was having to uproot Kim's mother. Readjustment to another country is usually not for the older person. I was justified in this concern.

We were fortunate in having a few friends in Italy, so I wrote for information as to what to pack. From Catherine I learned that glass and china were so reasonable that it was not worth moving ours. From Franco and Liliana (who had been in Deep River on an Italian exchange) I learned that warm coats and overshoes would be needed in a winter in the north of Italy. From Pina Beltrami in Genoa we were assured of a warm welcome. We had many loving letters from her during the eight months we were poring over maps and I was trying to decide what to take. As I packed and organized I often found myself dreaming of a green sauce she makes by pulverizing basil leaves with a mortar and pestle, *pesto alla genovese*.

I thought I was well organized but there was almost a scramble when train time came. However, I left our home without a qualm as we had wonderful luck in finding a tenant, a bachelor friend of ours who kept his house neat as a pin, and was keen to live down by the river. His cleaning lady came to me for a few weeks to see how I did things, and I knew our home was in safe hands. We stored a few larger pieces and our irreplaceable family albums, and left for New York on April 15th in a soft spring snowfall. We also left my suitcase in the garage. We did not notice this until we were checking our bags at the Chalk River station. Our tenant Jack drove us in and somehow, with three of us in charge and the snowfall, mine was put down and left. Our ship was late in leaving and Jack got the suitcase to us in time.

For weeks after this I would dream of Jack coming to our rescue in railway stations.

We were booked to travel on the Norwegian Concordia Lines "Tarek," with Captain Christianson, sailing from New York to Genoa. We had sailed with Concordia before on a trip from Genoa to Albany, New York. Concordia was a freighter line that is no more, and "Tarek" turned out to be a refitted "Liberty Ship." These all-welded vessels were turned out at the rate of one every day and a half by U.S. shipyards at the height of World War II. The all-welded hulls had a reputation for breaking in half under certain stresses. The hull had no flexibility, and a large wave lifting the vessel amid ships could cause a concentration of stress sufficient to rupture the plates holding it together. The first mate of the "Tarek" was philosophical about this. Such waves were rare, he said, and "Tarek" had been reinforced at the points of danger.

It is a feature of freighter travel that one is never quite certain when the ship will leave and when it will arrive at its destination. We discovered, upon arriving in New York, that "Tarek" would not be taking on passengers and would not be sailing for at least two weeks. We spent this time with Aunt Dorothy, who was now retired and living in the Chelsea Hotel, of artistic and literary renown, at 222 West 23rd St., in Manhattan.

We had arrived in New York on a Sunday morning. There was an important party that afternoon. It was the birthday of Miss Moore, the principal of the school Kim had attended in China, and the family was giving her a real celebration. My dress, so carefully pressed and packed for this party, was in my suitcase somewhere en route. Kim's two sisters had come for the party and to see us off and I was able to wear one of their dresses.

As soon as we knew that we were to go to Italy, we planned to travel by freighter if it could be arranged, as we knew it was our kind of travel. The fare is higher than tourist fare on a big ship, but since a freighter takes only twelve passengers (as it carries no doctor) you enjoy a freedom that cannot be allowed on an ocean liner. Every cabin has its own bathroom and portholes that open, since there is no air conditioning. This latter is a great selling point with me for I love to get my face in an open porthole. Why travel by sea if you can't enjoy it at any hour of the day or night? While I had my head out of the porthole, feeling the mystery of the sea late at night, I have seen some wonderful displays of phosphorescence and flying fish.

Anyone over seventy wishing to travel by freighter has to have a doctor's certificate to the effect that no trouble is anticipated during the trip. It was Mother's first trip by freighter and she was delighted with the spaciousness of her cabin. Truth to tell, they were really rooms, rather than cabins.

With so few passengers, you run the risk of having to put up with someone incompatible. Once more we were lucky, for we were a very congenial crowd. A newly retired university professor and president of an American college and his wife were off to Greece for a holiday. A young lady, a music critic for the Reader's Digest, was off to explore France. A young Italian mother married to an American was taking her two-year-old daughter, Pucci, home to visit her family. Charles, retired and a widower, planned to tour Europe by Vespa and carry on his hobby of tracking possible members of his family. A Vespa is a small motor scooter, well named after the wasp, for they are very fast and irritatingly noisy. Our freighter was calling at Las Palmas in the Canary Islands and the other three passengers were a mother from Texas going to visit her son and his family, and a mother and daughter returning to Las Palmas with the idea of settling there.

People who travel by freighter usually do so because they love the ocean and have time to take three or four days longer than the usual run. Also, if you have a great deal of luggage, there is always room to fit it in. There is no planned activity, and you have pretty well the run of the ship. You can sit for hours right up in the bow and watch porpoise cutting alongside with their incredible speed and grace.

On a big ship, the swimming pool has certain hours when it is open. On a freighter the pool is smaller, but you can swim before breakfast and in the moonlight before going to bed. You may even be allowed up on the bridge and have your hand on the wheel that steers the ship. You can go down into the engine room and see the huge propeller shaft turning, turning. Ever after, as I watched the bow cutting through the ocean or the stern wake bubbling out behind, I was conscious of that turning shaft. It had become for me the pulse of the ship.

We all ate at one large table with the Captain. We had previously discovered how good the food is on a Norwegian ship. If you are a lover of cranberries, then a Norwegian line is a must for you, as they are served three times a day. Mother celebrated her eightieth birthday on board and the cake provided was a masterpiece. No one could have wished for a livelier party. We had an equally happy one, two nights out from the Canaries when the Captain treated us to his party. At this party I met a drink called "acquavit." It is made in Denmark and it looks and seems perfectly harmless, but treat it with caution. If the bottle should have the picture of a ship on it, you know it has been aged in the hold of a ship, going from Denmark to Australia and back, as it is felt the motion at sea improves the acquavit. With or without a ship on the label, it is potent.

One afternoon we were all at the rail eagerly watching the shoreline of the distant Canaries become clearer. We docked in the evening, coming in slowly past many little boats fishing by the light of flares. The dock was gay – I might say garish – with quickly assembled booths guaranteed to make many of the sailors part with money. There were velour pillows of amazing colours with "Mother" embroidered in many languages. There were the largest dolls that I have ever seen and many lovely baskets and hats.

Five of us got our feet on dry land and taxied through quiet, almost deserted streets to a nightclub. The orchestra was so good you could not keep your feet still, but there was nothing spirited or intimate about the atmosphere. The building was as cozy as a large and impersonal railway station. I decided later that maybe it had to be vast for coolness sake in the hot season.

With only three hours' sleep, Kim and I stumbled out of our bunks at five the next morning to see what we could of the island before sailing time at ten. The warehouses down by the dock were already busy, the cargoes to go aboard being bananas, tomatoes and tuna fish. The bananas were small and green looking, but delicious. Some of the bright red tomatoes we knew had been grown on land down in the crater of an old extinct volcano. This is one of the island's showpieces.

As we walked we could feel that the place was usually sun-drenched. The buildings were mainly two-storey in a flat-roofed picturesque style. There is frequently a water shortage, so I presumed rain water was caught and stored by means of these flat roofs. The flowering trees and shrubs were exotic in colour and tropical in their profusion. The bougainvillea trees were great fountains just foaming over with magenta blossoms.

We walked the early morning quiet streets to one of the largest hotels, which was artistically adorned with carved wood. This carved wood is a feature of the island architecture and the wood goes so beautifully with the white or soft pastel shades of plaster. We had breakfast out in a lovely garden and overheard an English woman in difficulty with a waiter. She wanted more "buttah." Be prepared is always my motto. I had a Spanish phrase book. Kim and I spun the pages to "Useful Words". The first we found was "mountain goat" and we were rendered helpless with laughter. Maybe it was the fact that we had had so little sleep and were easily amused or maybe we were remembering an army phrase book that had a gem in the useful section: "our postilion has been struck by lightning".

We were no use to the English woman who was raising her voice, hoping to make the waiter understand. Later I realized the reason for her difficulty. An Italian that I met on a train told me that when he was going to England he knew the first word he would need was "porter," and he had it perfectly. When he arrived he was dismayed and lost when he heard people calling "poatah." Had the lady asked for "butter" instead of "buttah," I think the waiter would have understood. From my difficulties with Italian I know how exact you must be.

When you go ashore from a freighter you somehow do not feel like a tourist. Your ship is taking on cargo and you are ashore until it is ready to leave. After days of seeing just sea and sky, it was interesting to me that, in spite of the glory of the flowering trees and shrubs, we found ourselves drawn to the broad tiled walk along the ocean shore. The sweep of the waves was truly majestic. We were told that "Moby Dick" had been filmed in these very waters.

We made it back to the ship by ten and joined the others at the rail, watching two men throw enormous frozen tuna off trucks to be lowered into our hold. For three hours we chafed to be ashore exploring, as this painfully slow operation took place. Once the work was, or could be, in the hands of our crew all was speed and efficiency and I wondered how it was that the islanders could not find a speedier way of getting the fish aboard than hand throwing. Of course, it is to the advantage of the port, as the ship must pay for the time spent there. Even in those days it cost the Concordia Line $1000 a day to keep a ship in port. Captain Christianson told us that it was usual in Spanish ports for the entire staff of the customs office to come aboard. They were entertained with coffee and drinks at the table in the dining saloon. The captain then itemized the cargo and obtained permission to unload and load. At each customs officer's place at the table would be a carton of Chesterfield cigarettes and under the tablecloth an envelope containing U.S. dollars. This was expected. If omitted, the ship might be required to itemise everything on board, even half-cans of paint.

Our three new passengers were Americans, a young couple on holidays after a term of duty with an oil company, and a woman who had been visiting friends. It was fun to see their eyes light up when I passed around American chocolates. They felt it was not right to eat so many, but they could not resist. It is things like your own candy that you miss in another land.

From Las Palmas onward we seemed to be always watching something, the porpoise skimming by, Gibraltar in the early morning, the blue-purple rocky coast of Spain, and then Majorca way off in the distance. We had yet another gala Captain's dinner, and this time I treated acquavit with the respect it deserves.

We docked at Genoa on a clear, sunny day and had a fine view of the mountains that rise up behind the city. I was glad to see that the harbour was clear again. When the Germans left Genoa, they left the harbour unusable with sunken ships.

We were all excitedly eating our last breakfast on board, when Pina and Catherine were ushered in to join us for coffee. Also ushered in were a young aunt and uncle who started adoring Pucci the moment they saw her. On a big steamer you stand on board and your friends stand on the dock and you smile hysterically and wave frantically at each other. On this freighter we were able to hug our friends the moment we saw them.

It seemed an incredibly short time until we were all making our way to the customs shed. The first thing I noticed was that all the men gave us warm and friendly smiles as we made our way through the docking activities. I also noticed that all the trucks had two men, a driver and a man to replace him. There were bunk beds behind them in the cab, bright curtains, pictures, pin-up girls, a religious picture and even artificial flowers in some. After I found out how much Italians love to talk, I wondered if there had to be two men for conversation rather than for spelling each other for driving.

We soon had our first view of the traffic, which was flying by at an alarming speed. The vespas had us quite terrified and all of us, except Pucci, started to dissuade Charles from his idea of seeing Europe from one of these. It seemed to me he looked a bit shaken as we watched them darting through the traffic.

I was in none too confident a mood myself as I entered the customs shed. Coming across the ocean, we had all enjoyed an exceptionally beautiful azalea that our next-door neighbors in Deep River had sent us. Knowing our custom laws about bringing plants or seeds, I had thought to leave the plant for the Captain and crew to enjoy. Pina, busy organizing our departure, had popped it into a stout shopping bag. Very diffidently I held it up for inspection and heard a phrase I was to hear many times in Italy - "O che bella! Che bella!" meaning "how beautiful," and my plant was safely into Italy.

None of us had any customs delay, but as we said our goodbyes I was saddened to see the signs of strain creeping into the faces of our new friends. All our days at sea, the only decisions we had to make were what to wear and what and how much to eat. Now train connections had to be made, taxis procured and a different language coped with.

Catherine and Pina smoothed the way for us. A truck would take our luggage and be waiting for us in Varese. Unable to believe it could be this simple, we each kept a bag with us and I had my precious plant. Before noon we were on our train for Milan, and each of us had a *cestino*, a picnic lunch you could buy in the station. We heard it was Gracie Field's husband who invented this treat. It would contain salami or ham, cold chicken or breaded veal, rolls, cheese, fresh fruit, a small bottle of wine, a cup, a napkin and at least two toothpicks. No Italian meal is ever complete without toothpicks, and they are used often and assiduously behind a napkin held up to the face. A Canadian watching for the first time thought the man behind the napkin was getting ready to play a mouth organ, so you know it is a real maneuver.

There are diners on Italian trains, but for old times sake Kim and I were keen to have a *cestino* again. Our train was a *rapido* so we did not stop at every station, but I noted that every station had a fountain and flowers. I was also entranced by two ladies near us, who talked steadily, first one and then the other, and I do not think they ever looked out the window. As for us, we were practically glued to the window. Mother wanted to know why every station was called "*Uscita*" and, with great pride in my hard-won knowledge, I was able to tell her that "*Uscita*" meant "Exit."

The progress Kim had made in Italian really impressed me. When we got to Milan we had to taxi to another station and buy tickets for Varese, and he was able to take care of all our needs. He had made good use of our time on board and, while Pucci had her afternoon nap, he had profited by Nadia's willingness to help him with her mother tongue. I could have joined these sessions but knew that I would only hold up progress.

While we waited for our train, we treated Mother to her first *cassata* in the fine Motta restaurant adjoining the Stazione Nord. *Cassata* is a type of ice cream that I understand was invented in

Milan. The centre section is thick with peel and candied fruit and is surrounded with layers of different types of ice cream. As usual, there was the special ice cream spoon standing up in a glass of water. While we were enjoying this and watching the busy life of Milan streaming past, we were saddened by a well-nourished looking girl in her early teens who asked us for money.

There are two train lines from Milan to Varese, and we had chosen Ferrovia Nord as more convenient for us. At times this line takes on the characteristics of a bucking bronco. As we rocketed along, the speed did nothing to calm my mounting excitement. I had not expected any Italian train to be so eager to get me there. Neither had I expected the wisteria to be quite so beautiful. Some of it was a soft mauve, some of it was deep purple, but all cascaded down sun-baked walls and every spray had a beauty all its own.

Chapter 2

We Arrive in Varese

The city of Varese in those days had a population of about 70,000. It profited then, as it does now, from the wealth of Milan, only 40 km to the south. Varese nestles into the first of the foothills leading up to the Alps and is dominated by a mountain called "Campo dei Fiori," on the shoulder of which is situated the church of Santa Maria Del Monte. There is a famous pilgrims' walk up to the church with twelve elaborate chapels along the upward way, each of different architecture, each containing a depiction, in greater than life-size figures, of a station of the cross. The city is known to Italians as a *città giardino*, a garden city, for the wealth of Milan has led to the creation of beautiful public and private gardens throughout Varese.

Our destination was to be the Kursaal Palace hotel. The Kursaal had a long history as a luxury hotel and spa dating back to the late 1800s. It was used as a hospital and asylum during World War II, and was mistakenly bombed by the British, who were aiming for the nearby fighter plane factory, Aeronautica

Macchi. The damage to the hotel was still evident when we came to Varese, as was the ruined building (now a bank) across from the Hotel Europa in the middle of the city. These explosions were at least a kilometer apart. Pinpoint bombing was not in the R.A.F. book in those days. Aeronautica Macchi was untouched.

The Kursaal Palace was managed in our time by a Mr. Bizzi, whom we found in the garden of the hotel when we arrived, washing his car from an elaborate champagne bucket of soapy water. When I introduced myself in English and explained that we had reservations made for us by Euratom, his reply was "Not at all." My heart sank, as I interpreted this to mean that we had been stranded. It turned out that reservations had indeed been made, and that "Not at all" were the only English words he knew.

The Kursaal Palace has gone on to better things, and is now the "Palace Hotel" of Varese, a luxury hotel in every sense.

When we finally drew into the bright, cream-coloured station, I could hardly get off that train fast enough. At last I was going to see the city I had dreamed of for months, that I had tried to visualize and that I had looked at countless times on our maps. As we got into our taxi and drove to our hotel, what we saw delighted us. We passed old narrow winding streets with shops tucked in under arcades, then sections of ultra modern handsome architecture. Once more the traffic had me worried about Charles and his *Vespa* venture.

We were on our way to the Kursaal Palace hotel that had been leased by Euratom for single employees, and for married ones who were still hunting for permanent accommodation. It had been an ultra posh luxury hotel built at the turn of the century and was high on a hill-top. As our taxi snaked its way up that winding road, my heart went out to all the horses that in former days had strained their way up. Later I found an old defunct funicular that I fervently wished was still in use. The fine old trees and the lovely park made it easier, but the location of that hotel was for those who had transportation, not those who had been apartment hunting and had to climb on foot.

The view from the top is one of the finest in the city. Over to the west was the Lake of Varese. Interested as we were in gazing, at that moment the best view was the sight of our smiling truck driver and our small mountain of luggage. Many people had warned us of the difficulty of luggage transportation and almost certain loss, yet here was everything and smiles to boot.

When I travel I am not looking for what I have at home. I want the different and, believe me, I had it in that hotel. It was a palace by name and a palace in proportions. We stepped into a room of impressive size with handsome marble floors and great pillars. Our eyes ran up yards of glorious deep scarlet drapes. I found myself longing to share all this splendour with family and friends. If this was a hotel, what would be the grandeur of a real palace?

Our bedroom was another surprise. I was getting the different, all right! It was large and lofty. It had to be to accommodate the furniture that had definitely been there since the hotel was built. Every piece was large, sturdy and marble-topped. There were even bedside table cupboards complete with great porcelain chamber pots. The windows were doors opening onto a balcony, and over we went to have a really good look at the lake. The view of it and the mountains and villas was all we had dreamed it would be.

Whenever we had told people the part of Italy that was to be our home, they had all said "Oh, you will love it; it is beautiful there." Because of the beauty of this countryside and a climate that is much cooler than Milan, the wealthy Milanese have come here to build handsome villas and create lovely gardens. Kim and I stood there, well back on our balcony, for we both fear heights, quite lost in the beauty of the architecture, the gardens and the fine old trees. For me the beauty of Italy is as the beauty of mountains; you have to see it to fully comprehend its spell. No picture can do this for me.

I had been so eager to see the view that I did not notice that I was still holding our precious plant. I placed it where we could best enjoy it and turned with grave misgivings to investigate our bathroom. Our vintage furniture had me expecting real collector's items, but surprise, surprise! Although it was spacious enough to be a bedroom, it was ultra modern. The Italians know how to turn out the last word in smartness when it comes to bathrooms. Kim and I longed to bring home crates of their tiles.

As we unpacked, the old-fashioned furniture began to have an effect on me. I felt I should do my hair more demurely, maybe put a ribbon around my throat or put a fluff of lace somewhere. I really think anything would have been all right, for when we went down for dinner I had never seen so many hairstyles and completely different outfits. The idea with many European women (and definitely with Italians) is to be as much of an individual as possible. At first some of the effects, particularly in hairstyles, seemed fantastic to me. Remember it was 1962 and I had lived where uniformity was the general rule. Suddenly, I was in a world where the completely different was the goal to be striven for. I soon realized that plain women, by using heavy eye makeup, an unusual hairstyle and some clever trick in dressing, were able to create a real impression.

That night in the dining room I realized that European men also strive for the different. No two Frenchmen had the same haircut, and I had never seen so many styles in beards, not even in old family albums.

We listened to French, German, and Italian. This was to be our world for two years. When we had the chance to speak or hear English, it was a privilege and a treat. The coffee was a treat for Kim, who likes it strong, strong. Mother and I were inclined to share the view of an American who told us that the Italians were the only people he knew who had learned to melt the coffee bean. Fortunately, I grew to enjoy their brew, and Mother discovered *capuccino*. This is a coffee invented by the Capuccin monks; it is coffee with hot milk forced into it and often has a sprinkling of cocoa over it. But that night Mother had to down her strong potion. We then saw her up to her room under the eaves where, sad to say, even her bathroom was a vintage piece in all respects.

We phoned Franco and Liliana who, when they had been in Deep River, had come down to our place by the river. Now we were able to visit them and see their new young son. When I saw all the gleaming marble floors I wondered how Italian babies learned to walk without concussions; the floors looked so slippery and so much harder than wood. Naturally we were most interested to see everything, to give us an idea of what we might be living in. All the walls were plaster, the bedroom floors of wood and all the other floors of marble or tile. The balconies delighted us, but I wondered how with such high ceilings we would keep Mother warm enough in winter. There was a great exchange of news and I was able to ask the countless questions I had been storing up.

The next morning in Franco's car we were part of the procession of cars and buses making their way down that winding road from the Kursaal Palace hotel. The drive to Ispra was one of wonder and delight for us, past beautiful villas with spacious gardens, then through little towns with streets so narrow that only one car at a time could get through, then out into open countryside with people, mostly older folk, already at work in the fields. Throughout the drive, I had to get used to the honking of horns. Many routes in Italy were never intended for anything speedy, some not ever intended for motor vehicles. To make the streets wider would be to tear down the villages since the walls of the buildings are the sides of the road. When there is a right angle turn, all you can do to let anyone know you are coming is to sound your horn. Where possible, large mirrors are placed to let you see who is coming.

Ispra, the site chosen for Euratom, is a pleasant small village near Lago (Lake) Maggiore. On clear days, the snow-capped mountains on the Swiss border are so clear it seems they must be four miles away, not forty. We met all the people we should meet and then wandered around the vast grounds. Despite the many buildings completed, and the others being built, there was a great peace about the place on that sunny day in May. We were delighted to find a collection of picturesque old farm buildings being used as storehouses, spared by the bulldozer.

However, as a home was all-important, we cut short our meanderings and presented ourselves at the housing agency, an office in a group of apartment buildings outside the gates. The scientific buildings were all enclosed inside a fence with guarded gates. As time went on, and Kim checked on something in the laboratory after a trip, or on weekends, and I would be along in the car, I got to know these guards. And what ambassadors of good will they were! My heart still warms at the memory of their courteous, even gallant, manner of showing me into the waiting room, their patience with my halting and limited Italian, and then, when our car came in sight for the homeward trip, their manner of calling me.

In the housing agency we met a voluble Swiss-Italian lady who had all of Pina's energy and drive. She was able to talk rapidly in four languages. She took one look at us and said she had just the house for a childless, Canadian couple, a charming pagoda right on the shore of the Lake of Varese, ideal for "lake lovers." We were lake lovers, weren't we? Ha, she knew it, for we had the look of "lake lovers." Unfortunately there was one gentleman on the list ahead of us, but her tone implied that he could be dealt with. She gave us a list of other possibilities.

Magically, Franco appeared and drove us to a spot on the shore of Lago Maggiore not far from Laveno. For months I had been hearing and reading of the beauty of this lake. Oftentimes a thing falls short when it has been over-anticipated, but not

Lago Maggiore. However, we had to cut short our gazing and get on with finding a home. We clambered over construction material and in and out of unfinished apartments, trying to visualize what rooms would be like. The men working on these places were most pleasant and friendly but we realized nothing in this vicinity would be ready for months. The city of Varese would be our next try.

We lunched at a little restaurant in Laveno, eating outside under a trellis of vines. All round us was much talk and happy eating. I have never been able to decide which Italians would rather do, eat or talk, but I do know how much they enjoy both. This day we merged ourselves into the happy atmosphere and watched the activity of the port of Laveno, which is the starting point for cruises on Lago Maggiore. The railway station and the docks are side by side. I watched people hurry from the train to the waiting boat, never dreaming of all the people I would one day take on that tour.

Franco drove us as far as the town of Gavirate and left us by the bus stop for Varese. We stood under chestnut trees in full bloom, some white, some pink, and all in a mist of blossom. Soon a gentle rain started, and the blossoms came drifting down with the rain. Gradually, a small crowd gathered to catch the bus, and all had umbrellas. The first Italian lady to come was in black cotton, as are so many older women in Italy. She insisted on covering me with her umbrella. I managed to convey that she was getting wet for my sake and understood from her that my clothes might be spoiled by the rain and hers would not. This was the beginning of the kindness and consideration that I was to know in Italy.

The sun was out again by the time we reached Varese and Kim and I found our way around streets hunting for apartments. It was most interesting, for some buildings were hundreds of years old and others were spanking new. The city had been bombed in an effort to get the aircraft factory. Where a bomb left a hole, a new building went up. We soon realized there was no hope of finding a furnished apartment and we would be lucky to find anything. The enormous influx of Euratom people into the district had aggravated an already serious housing problem and we were beginning to despair of finding anything reasonable. However, we thoroughly enjoyed the singing of the workmen and the joking and byplay that went on as they tapped bricks into place and slapped on mortar. They all wore hats very neatly made from newspaper.

After the miles we had walked, the trek up to our hotel was almost too much, despite the beauty of the place. To live on that hilltop, a car was a necessity and ours was on order only. Poor Mother was completely marooned up there, no one to speak English with, and as it soon turned really chilly. She was miserably cold in those vast rooms. Our years in Scotland stood us in good stead, for we had learned to enjoy cooler temperatures.

Imagine our joy when the Euratom housing agent called and said we could have the house. It turned out to be a very attractive octagonal structure of two floors, with an outside stone staircase. This staircase was handsome in design and even when I had to descend it in the pouring rain to get something from the two downstairs rooms, I still loved it. The house was brand new, and was roofed with old, red, weathered tiles such as one sees on all the farmhouses and barns round about. This is a characteristic of Italy. It made the new house more a part of the countryside and at the same time probably saved a considerable amount of money.

Our pagoda house stood about fifteen feet from the shore of the lake of Varese, at the end of an open, unfenced field that had once been a vineyard. It was surrounded by all the trash and rubble of an unfinished house, but the agent for the house, who had supervised its building, assured us that the "systematisation" of the garden was merely a matter of time. He called our attention to the small rooms, the large radiators (a rarity) and the warm wooden floors of the upper story. Once more, we had met someone with amazing energy and animation. This was Signor Bruno Martignioni, who spoke rapid-fire Italian and Italian-French in a ringing voice that commanded our attention, even when we could only half understand what he said. Kim was sure he would have hooked us even if we had not liked the house. I did not like it; I loved it on first sight. All my life I had been fascinated by octagonal houses, and now I could live in one. It had a balcony as well. I knew Kim had dreams of an old villa in a lovely garden, but I was overjoyed to have a place that I could keep clean and where I could keep Mother warm. The house had oil heating, a most attractive fireplace, and the view of the lake was all you could ask for.

We had six weeks to wait until the place would be ready and decided to move into the old Hotel Europa in the heart of Varese. Before we moved, we had one of the best laughs in our lives. The Palace was slowly being modernized as far as bathrooms were concerned, and our room was on the edge of the modernizing process, so we heard all the banging and carryings on of the workmen. They were constantly calling out to a "Vittorio." I was feeling in fine fettle for I was loving Italy, and we had found a charming house. Every time I came into our room during working hours I called out to Vittorio, but very softly. One Saturday morning as I entered I could hear him tap, tap, tapping away and lo and behold he had tapped right in to join us. He was working down low and had not realized that an enormous hole was forming above. Our bed was covered with fine powdery white and more plaster was raining down with every blow of his trusty hammer. I beat a hasty retreat, found Kim and managed to get across to him that my calls to Vittorio had succeeded beyond my wildest dreams.

The scene that followed was hilarious. The maid and room boy (in Italy every hotel room was taken care of by a man and a woman) started to pound on the flimsy partition at the end of our hall. I knew a much quicker way to get Vittorio's attention, and invited them to our room. By now the hole was a really large one, and I stood on the bed and gave my last call. A pair of rueful brown eyes appeared and looked down in consternation at the *disastro* he had created.

We went off to make our arrangements to move into the Europa, and when we came back a few hours later all was plastered up and our room as clean as a pin. Nothing will dim our surprise and delight in having Vittorio make such a serious effort to join us. Those weeks in the heart of Varese were a boon to me, for I just had to learn some Italian in a hurry. Kim settled us in and then had to report to Brussels. He was back and forth, so Mother and I were dependent on me for ordering our food. Every day I studied the menu with my dictionary to give her some idea of what the dishes would be like. It is a real tribute to the Europa's kitchen that Kim and I do not remember a single meal that was not a real pleasure. It was a place we were always proud to take friends to for a meal. Sad to say, Mother did not share our pleasure in Italian cooking. Sad to say also, I cheated her out of ham, which she loved, because I did not know that *schinken* in German means ham. I thought our waiter was trying to say "chicken" in English, and Mother did not care for chicken. During those six weeks I did many things that I had never done before.

We were fortunate to move to the Hotel Europa. In those days it was run by the Stabilini family. The hotel is no more, and today the building houses smart, modern offices. It is on the Via Sacco, once part of the main carriage route from Milan to Ponte Tresa and Switzerland. Ponte Tresa today is only three-quarters of an hour away by car. The Europa was a stopping place in the old days, and when we lived there, still had a large carriage gate leading into a courtyard, which the Stabilinis had made into a garden. The stables and carriage shed had been converted into a gracious dining room, for which the Europa was famous. The kitchen was run by Signora Stabilini. An unmarried Stabilini sister managed the accounts. The family lived in the hotel and provided accommodation for Signor Stabilini's aged mother. This gave them something in common with us, since we had my mother with us. We became friendly with the Stabilinis, who, upon occasion, would invite us to dinner at their table in the dining room. They lived very well.

Chapter 3

We Settle In

I had to leave the task of settling in almost entirely to Kate. Working hours at the Euratom Centre were from eight in the morning to twelve noon, with two hours off for lunch. Work began again at two and continued until six, unless a meeting or some other event kept one later. I therefore had to leave our home in the morning not later than seven-thirty, and never got home in the evening before six-thirty. Kate took on this schedule with her characteristic enthusiasm and thrived on the challenge.

- - - - - - - - - - - - - - - -

I bought street maps and found my way to furniture stores. I, who had never dealt with a railway or a bus timetable, mastered both. My dictionary was never out of my reach. Previously, when I had tried to speak French in Switzerland, the Swiss always answered me in fluent English. In France, the French had dried up my French at the font by their impatience. The Italians gave me a wonderful confidence. They were kind and sympathetic. I was encouraged by *"Ma, la signora parla bene, parla bene!"* "But the Signora speaks well!" I knew it was not true, but I blossomed under the kindness, gained confidence and made progress.

I have since wondered if my early efforts in Italian were responsible for an adventure I had. I was investigating the possibility of second-hand furniture and had gone to a dealer. This dealer was over six feet tall, a real big chap. I will never know what I said or did, but suddenly I was swept into his arms and was being kissed violently and passionately. Even in my panic I remembered I was a Canadian in another land and did not want to let our women folk down in any way. I did my best in my weak Italian to tell him that perhaps our women, this one anyway, were not all that passionate. I was very happily married, etc. etc. I thought my cool but kind reaction would finish his ardour, but he was all for our going off together for the afternoon. I finally got away from him with my confidence in my Italian, and my confidence generally, sadly shaken. I was frightened at what might have been over-confidence in my scouting around the city alone. As I hurried back to the hotel, a dear old gentleman watering plants on his balcony gave me a courtly bow. I found myself thinking "Oh no, you don't; you old wolf, you." Then I took a look at his benign old face and things began to right themselves.

For a day or two I was rather cautious and suspicious. However, I was soon caught up in the warm friendly way of life and of doing business, and was scouting the stores again.

The light fixtures were supplied with our new house, but we had to supply the bulbs. I went to an electrical store. They did not have what I wanted but would send a boy off for it. They had just received their latest home movie from the developer, and while I waited, would I like to watch it with them? There I sat in the back of the shop enjoying their last holiday, watching the proprietor's *fidanzata* (fiancée), a lovely, long-limbed girl, cavorting on a beach while his beaming parents looked on. Shopping was never like this before. I was a stranger and did not know the city well, so they sent off for what I needed and supplied entertainment while I waited. With every encounter, I learned a few words and fell more in love with Italy and the Italians.

Life in the hotel was far from dull. I was making friends right and left. There was a *contessa* over ninety on the first floor. She had come to the hotel over twenty years ago and found it so pleasant she just stayed on. She did not leave her floor, but walked it with the regal bearing of a queen.

There was a Signorina Maria who spoke some English and who was in anguish trying to make up her mind to sell her family estate. It was too large for her to manage, but the wrench of breaking with so many old ties was almost more than she could face. Then there was Clara, who was saucy and provocative. I could not resist teaching her to say "So's your old man." It is the only English she speaks, but is guaranteed to bring the house down.

A movie should have been made of my trying to have a game of Scrabble with Mother and these two women squeezed in with us, the former fascinated with the English words she knew and questioning everything, the latter full of fun, and Mother desperate to get on with the game. I realized later that Clara was a prostitute.

Most of the residents in the Europa were people who had lived in the hotel for years, finding it more pleasant to live thus than cope with the practically impossible problem of trying to find help. They were of an age group that had grown up with servants and would have found it very difficult to learn to fend for themselves. And then the food was so good.

One older couple was there because their maid was in hospital for an operation. My difficulties with Italian verbs prompted Signora Maletto to introduce me to her son, who she knew could help me. What luck this was for us, for our association with Angelo, his wife Rina, and their three sons enriched not only our stay in Italy, but our whole lives. Our speaking English was good practice for them, and they were invaluable to us, as well as being wonderful friends.

I really think that Italians make the best friends. Their formality forbids easy and meaningless relationships, but once a friendship is established, it is for life. There is nothing an Italian friend won't do for you. You are part of the family.

I was getting to know all the people in the hotel, but Mother was isolated by the language. She felt drawn to one woman in particular, and since their feelings were mutual, they talked to each other, one in English, the other in Italian, with me trying to be the interpreter.

Then one rainy Saturday, who should come into the dining room but Charles. We had given him Franco's address and he had tracked us down. One trip across Rome on the back of a

Vespa had cured him of his idea of that kind of travel. Like Mother, he was finding it desperately cold and was not too happy with the food either. Now Mother had someone to talk to and even someone to make a fourth for bridge, as Kim was back from Brussels at the time.

Charles was keen to play golf, and I not only got him to the course, but managed to rent clubs. I was really proud of my Italian when I took him and Mother on the cruise on Lago Maggiore. This meant buying our tickets and working out the train and boat timetable. Lago Maggiore is the second largest lake in Italy and must be one of the most beautiful anywhere. For years, nobility and the wealthy have chosen to spend their summers there. The villas and gardens are lovely.

Although the first part of the trip on a car ferry lasts only half an hour, the Italian way of life – of enjoying life – means that the ferry is equipped with a bar and a small restaurant for light re-freshments and strong coffee.

At Intra, across the lake, you change to a smaller boat that takes you close into the shore, where you can enjoy to the full details of architecture and the beauty of the gardens. For this, my first trip, the rhododendrons and azaleas were in full bloom, and also the locust trees. As is the way with most white blos-soms, the perfume was incredibly sweet and heavy. When the breezes stirred the trees, the sweet fragrance drifted over the wa-ter to us.

There are stops at all the towns, and even the stops can be ex-citing, for the crew has to lasso mooring posts on the piers. Sometimes the rope misses and a second try must be made. The boat then heads away from shore, past a lovely little Madonna being lapped by the waves from the wake of the boat as she stands on a reef of rocks that would be dangerous to passing boats.

The first island is Isola Madre, famous for its gardens. The second is Isola Pescatori, where the fishermen who fish the lake have their homes and their picturesque boats. You can wander along the narrow streets here and feel time has stood still. The restaurants overlooking the water are small and simple but the food is good. I have never seen the island by daylight without at least one woman kneeling at the water's edge doing her washing. They kneel upon a specially prepared washboard arrangement with even a place for the big orangey-brown bar of soap.

Isola Bella, the most famous of the isles, was once a barren rock with a small church and a few cottages. In 1630, Count Charles the Third (of the noble Italian family of Borromeo, which still has extensive holdings in Italy) conceived the idea of transforming the island in honour of his lovely wife, Isabella. There is a palace surrounded by a garden of ten terraces, the lowest built on piles in the lake, and all decorated with statues and fountains. It is truly a riot of fancy. White peacocks strut amid the luxuriance of rare exotic plants. These peacocks spread their tails often enough to have photographers on their toes. All the soil for these gardens was brought from the mainland. Having laboured long and hard to have a garden in the sandy soil of Deep River, this transportation of soil was of great interest to me.

The palace has fine furniture, tapestries and ancient weapons, and of course a bed where Napoleon once slept. I do not envy Napoleon the beds he slept in, but I do envy him the beautiful spots he chose for slumber. With every visit to that palace, I thought what a dream come true it would be if I could just once sleep in that bedroom lapped by the lake, and wake to the magnificent view of the mountains.

The grotto rooms particularly intrigued me. They are just above the water level and are like caves all walled with shell and volcanic rock. I assumed they were to retire to when the heat of summer became intense. There is also a room where, in April 1935, Ramsay MacDonald, Sir John Simon, Pierre Laval and Eugène Flanden met, summoned by the League of Nations to challenge Hitler's act of treaty violation.

Stresa is the last stop on this travel tour. The shops here are a delight and it is from Stresa that you have the best view of the lake and the islands. There is great charm about its villas and gardens. In hydrangea time it is a must if you are anywhere near. It has long been a favourite spot for travellers and Italians alike.

The sun shone brilliantly for this, my first conducted tour. Mother got quite a sunburn. During most of these days, though, the weather was exceptionally cool, which was most unusual, so everyone said. Finding no word in my dictionary for hot water bottle, I went to a store and explained that *mia Mama* was cold, and I wished hot water for her bed. It worked like a charm. There was a beam of understanding and a hot water bottle was mine.

Not only was the weather cold, but I was surprised at how often it rained. Italy produces some of the best rainwear and umbrellas in the world, and I was beginning to realize why. I have never known a people so respectful of rain. With the first drops, up go the umbrellas, and then commences the battle of who shall raise his and who shall lower his on streets or sidewalks so narrow that two umbrellas cannot pass. Fishermen fish from under umbrellas, goat herders watch their flocks (or their one goat) from under one. The head and shoulders are protected, but I never saw one pair of rubbers, no matter how heavy the deluge. Instead, men and women wore platform wooden sandals to keep their feet above the wet. They are very clever at riding bicycles and managing an umbrella, and I used to marvel at one man who contrived to read his paper, hold up his umbrella, and control his bicycle, all in Italian traffic.

A sunny day, after days of rain, brings out a crop of umbrellas hung upside down on the clothesline. When we were on a trip, I could always tell if the district had been rained on the day before by the sunning umbrellas.

Despite all I was seeing and doing in Varese, my thoughts were on our new home and I made many bus trips out to see how things were progressing. On my first trip I asked for information at the bus station, and the person I asked led me to the bus and made sure that the driver knew just where to let me out. As we approached the stop, there was a concentrated effort of all passengers to get me off. I only hope we are as kind and helpful to strangers in our land.

The bus stop was right at the end of our lane and then I had a short walk down the lane between a fine old barn and a little stream.

To take Mother and Charles out to see our house, we rented a car. It was a brilliantly clear day and for the first time we saw the mountains out in all their glory, and they were all snow-capped.

It seemed too good to be true that on clear days we would have a view like this.

Charles was captivated with our *sitz* bathtub in the tiny downstairs bathroom. This is a very small tub where you sit on a seat with your knees bent. The advantage is that, although you have no space to stretch your legs, you can be immersed in water up to your armpits without using as much water as in a normal tub, and you can have a sitz bath in a place too small for a normal tub. Charles was so fascinated with it, I had visions of him taking one back to the States.

During our stay in the city, when Kim would be back from Brussels, our evenings would be full after the Scrabble game. I had to take him to see an especially beautiful wrought iron gate, or a fountain, or a fine old lamp. I soon discovered in Italy one must look through every arch, as there can be lovely surprises: gardens in inner courts, or charming little statues posed in a fountain. After our evening wanderings, we would join the sidewalk café crowd in the Piazza Monte Grappa. Every city or town in Italy has its *piazza*, and here you sit outside and eat ices or sip drinks and enjoy the fountain and watch the crowd. A most popular Italian pastime is watching people.

Italians adore their children, dote on them, and would not dream of trusting them to a babysitter. When they enjoy a drink in the moonlit *piazza*, their young are with them. I have often seen children out as late as eleven, playing about or sitting with their elders and being unbelievably good.

Most Italian mothers will agree to leave their children with a relative, but no one else. I have heard some of the husbands plead with their wives to try a babysitter, but cannot bring them to it. A couple will bring their child with them to your home. At first I worried about these late hours for children, but when I found how long the afternoon siesta lasted, I worried no more.

Across from our hotel was a large, rather impressive building, in that soft, warm creamy colour that is just off terra cotta and that goes so well with Italian sunshine. I discovered that, though it is now the *municipio*, or municipal government offices, it had been a palace of Francis, third Duke of Modena, had taken years to build, and had been started in 1768. The Stabilini family, who were in charge of the hotel, said I must be sure to visit the gardens. I went across the street to investigate, totally unprepared for the acres of garden and the magnificent old trees. You have to see huge cedars of Lebanon to appreciate them. There was a fountain fit for a duke, waterfalls, and walks completely covered by old beech hedges. I sat on the bench and watched mothers or grandmothers watching their young. I was constantly amazed at how beautifully the children were dressed and how clean they kept themselves. Old ladies used to come every day the sun shone, and worked away at knitting or sewing, and how they talked. The size and beauty of those gardens came as such a surprise to me that I loved to recommend visiting the garden to strangers, and then enjoy their surprise and delight.

The Stabilini family consisted of a beloved older mother, a married daughter who supervised the excellent kitchen, and an unmarried daughter and son who ran the business end of the hotel. The latter two spoke some English, and from them I learned that our hotel had been a stop on the old stage coach route from Milan to Lugano in Switzerland, and that it had been built in 1840.

I found this very exciting news and pelted up the stairs, bursting in on Mother with "Mother this hotel was built over a hundred and twenty years ago!"

Said Mother, rather tersely, "I can well believe it." Then we burst into giggles for I had given her the perfect opening. All was wonder and interest for me, but she was cold and longing for the food and things she had known at home. Charles had left, Kim was away, and she had only me to talk to.

Now I understood the huge size of the dining room. In the early days it had been the coach house for the hotel, and what now made exceptionally large French doors into the hotel's inner court garden had been the doorways for the stage coaches.

Just around the corner was a quaint old courtyard where countless wheels had worn deep grooves in the old stone. Paintings of men of a bygone age, in all their finery, look down from the walls. I never found out who they were, but the interesting old hardware store that formed part of the business of that quiet courtyard was housed in the cells of a monastery that gave a retreat for monks in the late 900s.

Due to its location, its beauty and its summer climate, Varese is a popular spot for conventions. The first that came and filled the hotel was a worldwide poultry convention. We met two charming Israelis, Leah and Yudah, and their sunbeam of a daughter. Israel had done so well in poultry raising that they were now showing the Italians how to set up similar systems. Now we are far more knowledgeable about poultry and life in Israel.

All the booths were set up in the grounds of the Varese villa that had once belonged to the Ponti family. We had a special interest in going, for our Lake of Varese had belonged to this family. There had been very exciting parties on the lake, and even a gondola to bring the merrymakers over to the island. Now all that remains of these nights of gaiety is the slightly crumbling pavilion on the island, the handsome iron ring where the gondola was tied to the stone steps leading out of the water, and a boathouse on the mainland. This boathouse is still a most attractive building. Out of the upper floor, where folk waited to be ferried over to the island, our agent, Signor Bruno, had made an apartment that would have interior decorators green with envy. In the lower part of the building, where the gondola floated, he now had a small fleet of motorboats for the water ski club he operated in summer.

I think that Kim and I were the two most eager people who went through the gate to the Ponti's residence. The clucking hens and the crowing roosters and the poultry equipment were of the finest. But we felt privileged to have the chance to visit the home and gardens of the family who had given us our lake. The villa had the proportions and grandeur of a small palace. The walls of many of the rooms were beautifully painted from floor to ceiling with scenes that were a mystery to us. The gardens, the huge old trees, the cool stone grottos and the waterfalls had all the beauty we had expected of Italy. When we saw our flag flying among those of other participants, we had a thrill of deep pleasure and pride, and a real twinge of homesickness.

The next event that came along was a dog show. This was a real surprise, for we had seen no person with a dog on a leash, and not even a dog on the streets. In Lugano, in Switzerland, many people walked their dogs, but the only dogs we had seen in Italy were watchdogs chained near the doors of houses in the country. However, the dog show was very popular and our hotel was filled to overflowing for the three days that the dogs were on display in the gardens across the street. The Stabilinis even allowed dogs in the dining room. The normal peace of dining was gone, for from under the chairs of dog owners came menacing growls every time the waiter's feet came near. Whenever a new dog arrived, there would be a wild slithering of toenails on the tile floor as a charge was staged.

Incidentally, all the judges were English. When I realized how keen the competition was, I decided that being a judge at a dog show must be very difficult.

When the dog show left, peace once more descended on the hotel. Outside, the traffic roared by and had to be heard to be believed. The quiet in the hotel was disturbed only by soccer matches on television. I had no idea that soccer was so popular in Italy. When a match was on TV, no male guest was in the dining room. At a burst of wild cheering, the waiters would either drift, or dart, out to see if they could get a glimpse of the action. One very keen fan on the outskirts of Varese painted his villa with stripes in the colours of his favourite Milan team.

It is the custom in Italy to have the two rival teams arrive the day before the match and stay at the same hotel. We sat through some pretty tense meals on the day of the match, with one team at one long table, and, across the dining room, the other team. It was not unpleasant tenseness, more the feeling of an athlete waiting for the gun to go off so the race could start.

The team members would often throw rolls at each other in horseplay to let off a little steam. Mother found the hard, crusty rolls not to her liking, and with a chuckle told us she was sure these athletes had found their true use. The enthusiasm in the hotel prepared me for later happenings. When an umpire had to be spirited away and hidden from the crowd, it was not such a shock to me. When Bologna beat Milan in the playoff, and was accused of winning with doped players, I could understand why all cars bearing a Milan license plate were forced to fly the Bologna colours if they hoped to move in Bologna streets.

Most of my daylight hours were spent in the streets, and here one had to accustom oneself to being stared at. It was not just the men who seem to take in every detail, but the women too. For some foreigners this is disturbing, for there is no pretence about it. They look you right in the eye. When we had first visited Genoa, I had been disturbed by this staring and had questioned Catherine about it. Her answer was, "If they stop staring, then you had better start worrying." Men driving by express their approval by a little toot on the horn. You can even be with your husband and receive an "Okay". One morning, as I walked over to the *piazza* with Kim, I must have met with one man's approval, for he said right out "O, la la!" Kim murmured, "Home was never like this."

I was never pinched but I had an American friend who was. She was so furious she threw a stone at the man. I would have loved to have seen his face. He was paying her a compliment and she replied with anger.

As I hunted for furniture, I would often slip into the Basilica San Vittorio, which was started in 1580. I would pray and then sit and enjoy the elaborate wood carving and be awed by the Baptistry, dating from the twelfth century. I was drawn there as it was off in a quiet square with a charm all its own. Guests visiting us later told me this square and the church could have come straight from Mexico. I interspersed my furniture hunting with my delight in the rose filled gardens and the beauty of the wrought iron gates.

As I shopped and explored, I realized a great change was taking place in me. I had always had, as I think many Canadians have, the feeling that it is almost wrong to enjoy oneself too much. One has almost a sacred trust to be busy justifying one's existence. The Italians, on the other hand, have learned how precious is the enjoyment of the moment. They have a great capacity for living and taking pleasure in life. Later as I tried to understand why they had the qualities I admired and others that I did not, I realized that, as their history had been one of so much siege and conquest, they had to develop this capacity for living to the full in the moment. In those first days it was getting through to me even though I did not understand the why of it. I found myself stopping at sidewalk cafes to enjoy the street scene. I remember one day setting out with my map to find a furniture store. I was having trouble and sat down on a stone bench to find my street. A heavy, older man eased himself down beside me and offered to help. I soon realized that all he was doing was enjoying the map, and savouring the recognition of streets that he knew. I had thought I was in a hurry, but I had come to that part in my Italian indoctrination where his enjoyment of my map was far more important than anything that I thought I had to do.

One day, while Mother and I were having lunch, I was called to the phone. It was Signor Bruno's sister, and she gave me the feeling that my Italian was not so bad after all. She greeted me with "I speak English. Good evening." The hot noonday sun was beating down, but I gamely said, "Good evening." When she said, "I am my brother's wife," I did not know just what to say. Then she said, "Your house is now ready." That made real sense to me. Now my dream-like stage of Italian life had come to an end. Now I must find our food and keep a house clean.

Those six weeks we had at the old Hotel Europa, I realize now, were God-given. They allowed us to become accommodated to life in Varese without the responsibility of looking after a house and providing meals. By the time we moved down to the lake, Kate had gained confidence in her ability to manage in Italian, and to deal with travelling on buses and shopping. By the time the house was ready for us, we had received delivery of our car, a Fiat 1100 *Familiare*, a tiny station wagon with a tiny motor. A car was absolutely essential for getting to work at the Centre. There was no bus service that passed our house (the Italians called it a *villa*) that went on to the Centre. There was a regular bus service connecting us with the city of Varese, and Kate made good use of this.

Chapter 4

We Move to the Lake

The Lake of Varese is not so famous as its neighboring Lake Maggiore or Lake Como, but it has always played an important role in the history of the region. Nestled into the foot of the mountain called *Campo dei Fiori* that dominates the region, it lies just south of the city of Varese. It is roughly the shape of a foot, the toe being the eastern extremity of the lake and the ankle being at the western extremity. The distance between them is about nine kilometres. Our house still stands, and is on the north shore of the lake at about the arch of the foot.

- - - - - - - - - - - - - - -

The weekend we moved, our car most conveniently arrived. We had been so impressed with the speed of drivers and the wildness of traffic that we had ordered a red car that "would not show the blood stains." But everyone must have had the same idea, for we had to settle for a white car.

When it came to buying our supplies, I felt none too confident of my amounts in grams and kilograms. I asked Silvia (the maid on our floor, and by now our dear friend) if she would come with us on our first shopping expedition. This proved to be a wonderful bit of luck. We went to the *cooperativo*, a store in Calcinate, the little village closest to our home. I had my list of the essentials all made out, and Silvia told them how much we needed. To my surprise, we had to go to the *tabaccaio* for our salt and matches. This is a shop that sells tobacco, stamps and always has a bar where you can buy drinks and coffee. In my ignorance, I thought this was a way of spreading business around in a tiny village. Later I found out these articles were government taxed and were sold in the *tabaccaio* where the high tax on tobacco was collected.

The *tabaccaio* was on the corner of the main street and was run by a Signora Zanetti and her son. We pushed aside the curtain of fine beads to witness a scene typical of Italy. On seeing Silvia, there was a cry of joy and the two women were in each other's arms, kissing each other on both cheeks. It turned out that they had once been ill in the same ward of the hospital. In no time we were in a back family room having coffee. The beautiful young granddaughter, Giovanna, had run to fetch her mother, who ran a shop that supplied the local people with dry goods and clothes. The other daughter came from her shop, a *casalinga*, or general store for pots, pans, glass plates, etc. Now we had our entrée into the life of Calcinate, and how lucky we were! Through this family we got to know many of the local people. We never passed through the village without a warm smile or a wave from someone. The Italian wave is the complete opposite of ours. You hold up the hand, palm towards yourself, and close it as though beckoning the person toward you with the whole hand. It is hard to change a well-established habit like a hand wave, and for quite a while mine was a wildly convulsive thing, as I would realize suddenly it was wrong. I must not wave, but beckon.

While our stay in Varese had been a wonderful experience, we were happy to have more than our hotel rooms for private living. With the heat had come clouds of large miller moths that had created a real problem. If we left our great shutters open, we could hardly see across the room for moths. If we shut the moths out, then we kept the cool evening breeze out too. We were glad to get away from the steady din of the traffic to the peace of the country. We were enjoying our bright bare rooms and the breeze from the lake. Oh, we were fast falling in love with our new home.

However, our love affair with the lake did not begin without a hitch; in fact, there were several hitches. We arrived during a climactic phase in the life cycle of a small, winged insect which seemed to have no other purpose than to fly into the house (screens are unknown here in the country), cling to the ceilings for a day and then fall dead to the floor. Every morning there were feathery mounds of these creatures in every corner and angle of the house, smelling faintly of decay. There were of course other insects. Kim developed an almost pathological hatred of earwigs. Mother's hate was of an insect we never caught in the act, but one that left small, conical mud cocoons in shirts, between blankets, anywhere where he had privacy. But wonder of wonders, there were no mosquitoes. Even the bees and wasps seemed to have a benevolent tolerance of humans. We know, as they had free access to the house. A characteristic of life in Italy seems to be mutual tolerance between man and insects; a state of affairs which results, however, in a pretty high average concentration of moths, ants, gnats and beetles of all shapes and sizes. At first I found cooking difficult with bees often flying about me, but when I never got a sting I soon learned to ignore them. The compensation of not having to open a screen door to stroll out on the balcony made the endurance of insect life easier. Somehow it made the outdoors so much more a part of your life.

The second hitch we noticed during our first visit to the house. Our front lawn (to be) appeared to be a favourite haunt of fishermen. Signor Bruno assured us that they would not come once the house was occupied. How wrong he was! They came even from as far away as Milan, arriving at 5:00 a.m. on popping Vespas and motorcycles, coming to a noisy stop right outside our bedroom balcony. A fence was put up, a gate closed and locked, but still we had fishermen, on foot now, but still fishermen. Kim spoke firmly but kindly to one on our lawn, who said, with disarming charm, "Where would you expect me to fish, on a mountain?" We tried at all times to keep firmly in mind that we were Canadians and that Canada might be judged by what we said. At this point Kim told him he didn't care where else he fished, but it was not to be from our front lawn.

We then went into the house to finish some shelves we were constructing. "Building" is too mild a word to apply to the weight of the wood we were working with. We had bought it from Signor Giamberini, who ran the local sawmill. We were delighted with the picturesque water wheel his father had built many years before. While he now used municipal electricity for power, he was always willing to set the old wheel going whenever we walked over with friends. The lumber is cut in planks the shape of the tree and still has the bark on. When stacked around the mill, this manner of cutting keeps you conscious of the trees that supply the lumber.

Whatever type of lumber we had bought, it was almost as heavy as lead. After working on our shelves for about twenty minutes, we looked out, and there was that same fisherman back in the same spot on our front lawn. Kim tore down our outside stairs. This time the fisherman told him there were no signs telling him not to fish. Kim ground out through clenched teeth: "Well, there soon will be," and in no time our place was bristling with "No Fishing" signs. Still they came, climbing over the fence, wading out past a series of posts, even mooring their boats on our wall.

I came to the conclusion that many Italians have no respect for private property or privacy. We could be eating on our front balcony and one or two would quietly filter in. Only a great roar of "Via! Via!" would get them to move. I wondered if perhaps they would welcome us on their property and saw no reason why they should not be welcomed on ours.

The third hitch was the "systematization" of our garden. It was clearly going to be a matter of years. Signor Bruno, our agent, would shake his head sadly over the *disastro* and complain that he could get no one to do the work. Everyone was either working their farms or had gone to the factories.

We eventually bought garden tools and set to work ourselves. Gradually, during the summer, the garden began to take shape. Our azalea flourished on the shadier side of the house, and all the plants I bought at the market seemed to love their new home. Kim learned to swing a scythe like the farmers in our district as our grass gradually grew to cutting length. We could have bought a lawn mower, but he preferred the quiet swish of the long curved blade.

Our house had been built as a summer place for a Swiss family in Lugano and was compact. It had built-in clothes cupboards in the bedrooms upstairs. This is quite rare in Italy, as families have to move clothes presses about with them. We also paid extra rent to have the kitchen completely furnished. An Italian kitchen is supplied with a sink and the tenant must supply all else, even the cupboards, which are usually of metal.

The furniture I had scouted out in Varese fitted in very well. It was always a pleasure to me as I had had such a pleasant time buying it. Everyone seemed to understand perfectly my desire to spend as little as possible; we would need it for only two years. I found Italians like the Scots in their respect for money and their desire to help. Frequently, shopkeepers pointed out ways I could save, and once a greengrocer refused to sell me a salad green that was newly on the market and expensive, explaining that I could use something else just as good and not so dear.

We had brought one rug for the living room, some light curtain material and some Canadian paintings, mostly from the Group of Seven. Our home soon had a cozy look, especially when our grate fire was burning. With all that marble, an Italian place can look elegant, smart and sophisticated, but seldom cozy.

We spent about three hundred dollars on furniture. After much looking, I bought most of it at one large store that allowed us a fifteen percent discount because we were from Euratom. Our chairs were the wicker type used in sidewalk cafes, and cost five dollars and ten cents each. They served as balcony chairs as well. The dining room chairs and the table had to be light and easily moved for balcony meals. The chairs were wood with cleverly woven plastic seats. The table was one of our major expenditures, costing all of forty dollars. A few small wicker tables with sophisticated black iron legs, and that heavy bookcase we had made, finished our living room. We could furnish in this rough, rustic style because we were in the country and by a lake. It would have looked strange in an apartment in Varese. The wooden floors, our Canadian pictures, and the fact that no Italian would think of using wicker sidewalk cafe chairs, always brought forth exclamations of *"una casa canadese!"* "A Canadian home!"

We were fortunate that Mother had taken up patchwork quilts as a pastime, for ours were much admired and were so typically North American. I bought the cheapest of bedsprings of the type used by schools. Italian mattresses are light and easy to move because they spend a good part of the day out in the sun. Every sunny morning, beds are stripped and mattresses hung out the window, over the balcony. Often, on one of our trips, after we had stayed at a small hotel, I would turn for a last look back and see the green shutters of our room thrown open and our mattresses thrown over the sill to hang like long tongues in the sunshine.

Two men and one small truck delivered our furniture in many trips. This truck consisted of a framework on a small motorcycle. Already, I had learned not to expect the speed and efficiency we demand on our side of the water. There were compensations for me, real ones. Those two chaps were warm, happy human beings. They delighted in our view, our unusual, compact house, and Mother's Mitch Miller records. They hung my two door-length mirrors. These cost nine dollars each. Mirrors were very reasonable, but in my drive for economy they were to take the place of dresser mirrors. They also cut down the legs of the dining room table so it would look more a part of the living room. There was no charge for this. They had enjoyed the music and the view.

I had heard many tales of tourists being cheated, so I was prepared for it, but to my knowledge I never was. It always seemed to me that Italians as a whole were exceptionally helpful, and maybe my desperate floundering in Italian brought out all their friendliness and kindness. Before these chaps left, they did me one more service. I wanted to know what our exact address should be and they drove me up to the main road, went to a house, and found out for me that our lane, Via Duca degli Abbruzzi, was the dividing line between the municipalities of Varese and Gavirate.

We were phenomenally lucky to have two bathrooms, but they were so small that there was no place for a washing machine, and there was no laundromat in town. I investigated laundries, prices and the length of time things would be kept. I was already aware of the uncertainty of its being ready when promised. I came to realize that one of the prices I was going to have to pay for living in my beloved house by the lake was that I was going to have to do our laundry by hand.

I was never able to find a hand wringer but gradually evolved quite a laundry system with our half-bath downstairs. Either my system was good, or it was all due to Italian sunshine, but my wash was white, white.

When I would get letters from friends in Deep River envying me my life in Italy, I wondered if they would envy me my laundry facilities. An American woman in Euratom confided to me that she nearly fainted when she asked to see the laundry room and they showed her the bathtub.

In Ispra, the supply of women available for domestic help was good, but out where we lived, all the women either worked on farms or in factories. So I had the satisfaction of not only keeping our house clean, but of doing our laundry by hand, and sometimes by feet. Since many of the local women who had access to the lake washed in it, I thought "When in Rome...etc." In nice weather, I rinsed in the sunshine at the lake, enjoying the birds and watching the passing fishermen. The first time I recall being together with three other Canadian wives, all from Deep River, two of us confided to each other that, due to washing over the bathtub, we had discovered back muscles we had never known we possessed.

In the villages of northern Italy, there always seems to be a stream hurrying through, and every village had its washhouse. This was a stone or stucco structure open on one side, sometimes on all four. The stream ran through a series (or through at least two) vast troughs. Here the village women did their wash, talking as they scrubbed, beat, beat and pounded. They used only a bar of soap and their wash was pure white. They carried the wet wash home on their heads, or in their arms, or two friends would help each other, but I never saw a cart used. Sometimes, off in a field, a long way from any dwelling, we would see a trough, like a small, shallow swimming pool, open to the sky, fed by a spring. Not only did some women walk a long way to do their wash, but also to hang it up, if there was no good drying location near their house.

In some of the villages there was no running water in the homes. Then you would see children and older people going to the village fountain or tap. When we were on trips in the mountains and were nearing our evening destination, I loved to see the healthy, brown-faced children swinging along to the fountain for the night supply of water.

When we moved into our new house, it had been over two months since I had prepared our meals, and it was not easy to start again. There were many items I could not find at first, and some I never did find. I had always taken brown sugar for granted. If I found it in Italy, I considered myself very lucky. Switzerland, only forty miles away, proved a source for hard-to-find items. Naturally, prices on imported things were high.

We Canadian women were very sorry for one of our group. She had been overjoyed to find candied fruit (she thought) in a *salumeria* (a delicatessen). She hurried home and made a special type of cake. As it baked, she wondered where the strong smell of garlic was coming from. Sad to say, it was from her own oven.

The Italians eat this type of fruit highly spiced as a relish with meat. She did not have many takers for that cake.

We all worked out a system of shopping and getting along without the things we could not have, but there were times when your mouth watered for some favourite food. There were odd things you longed for, such as cottage cheese, sour cream, and the convenience of baking chocolate.

Our kitchen was so tiny – just six feet by eight – that real contriving was necessary. As well as the fridge and the stove, there was a *bombola di gaz*, a cylinder of propane gas for the stove. The cylinder had no way of letting me know when it was about to give out. It frequently did at the most inconvenient times. Then, to quiet my frustration, I had to remind myself of the beauty of our view and how much I loved to listen to the silvery notes of the church bells coming over the water. Luckily, the sink was a double one, and Kim made me a covering for one half that gave me a little counter space. When I baked or had guests, there had to be real planning and organization in that pocket handkerchief of a kitchen. My only real disaster was when, having absolutely no place to put an iced birthday cake, I had to put it on the floor and, a moment later, stepped into it.

Shopping was not as much of a surprise to me as it was to most North Americans, for in Britain I had learned to go to a different store for different items. The *cooperativos* in the country carried a supply of your generally needed items, but the choice range was small, especially of fruit and vegetables. These stores carried very little meat. In Italy you go to a bakeshop, a meat store, a fruit and vegetable store, and a store called a *drogheria* for your staples, ranging from sugar and flour to almonds and raisins. Very few items were packaged. Great canisters were brought down and your purchase twisted up into a spill of paper, or a cone. If you wished bacon, butter, cold meat, etc., off you went to a *salumeria*. Just to stand and gaze into one of these is a treat in itself. The Italians are real artists at arranging food and fruit. Another call had to be made to a *latteria* for milk and cream. Butter and cheese could be bought here or in a *salumeria*. Coffee, tea and cocoa were bought in another shop selling only these items, and every time you ran out of salt or matches you had to find a tobacco shop.

These trips to the different shops were very time-consuming and had to be fitted into the bus schedules. Kim wondered about a second car for me, but I wanted all our extra money for sight seeing. After a few bus trips, I realized they were a wonderful way to get the feel of our part of the country, for everybody talked and there was much fun and byplay.

The summer heat was so strong now that it seemed to bounce right back off the walls of the buildings. When I discovered that "Standa," the department store in Varese, had our type of supermarket in the basement, it solved my hot weather shopping. Standa was an absolute boon to the newcomer. It was a very modern chain of stores carrying all your needs, with all the prices in sight. All you had to do was point and produce your money. I had visited it nearly every day while at the Europa, but never knew the basement was a supermarket. Here I was able to buy eggs in cartons. Oh joy! Oh joy! No more trips home on the bus with a fragile paper bag of eggs. I remember one rainy day, making my way to the bus along the narrow streets, dodging umbrellas and clutching my bag of eggs, icing sugar oozing gently out of its paper cone, and I was sucking a caramel that had been part of my change at the bakeshop. (This was a standard practice if the shop did not have the correct change). I thought "well, you wanted the different, and you are getting it."

Many things were a surprise to us. It seemed an absolute impossibility for Italian electricians to get light fixtures flush with the surface of ceilings. Somehow Kim achieved a perfect job on ours that was the envy of all who came to our house. However, when we went to hang a picture under a light, I cautioned that it might be dangerous so near the wiring. He said "Look, Kate, every wire is safely enclosed in heavy duty conduit." Things were different in our house, for when he drove in the nail, there was a blinding flash and we were without power until Kim replaced the fuse.

One of the different things I had to get used to was lizards. A lovely feature of our house was a poplar tree that had been left to grow up through our front balcony, protected by an iron ring that matched the attractive iron railing. We loved this tree, but it made a perfect way for lizards to sun themselves on our balcony and take reconnoitering trips into our house. They could come up the walls, but the tree made it easier. At first I was afraid they might get shut in, but we learned to live together. Kim and I became quite fond of the small type, but were a bit leery of the larger (*ramarro*) type we saw in the fields, for they leapt along in a way too fast for comfort. One day Kim came home from work and gave me three guesses as to what he had found in his filing cabinet. I guessed a lizard on my first guess. When I walked along our country roads, I got so used to them rustling about in the dry roadside that I missed them when the cold weather came.

Our guardian angel was really on her toes during our stay in Italy. So many things just fell into place in a perfect way. Up on the hillside in the smaller of two soft yellow villas lived the Bottinis. They could have been aloof and unfriendly, but either our guardian angel or good luck saw to it that they were people who gave us a second home. We were welcome any time. They loved sharing TV shows with us and seemed to understand how much it meant to us to be able to show Canadian guests an Italian country villa.

We were unable to get a telephone because the system was overloaded. If Signora Bottini found out, as she sometimes did, that Kim had put in a call from Gropello, I would receive a reproachful scolding and be called *cattiva, cattiva* (naughty or bad) for not using the Bottini phone.

This complete sharing of their home with us is quite unusual in Italy. Many foreigners are entertained but usually in a restaurant. When you are invited to a home, you realize to the full what hospitality is, but the home is not thrown open as it is in the U.S. and Canada. It is reserved for family and old friends. Being one of a large family, this feeling of real welcome was very precious to me.

Since the road to Calcinate was twisty and narrow, and the stretch of road to the Gropello cooperative store in the other direction was wide and straight, I had decided to register at Gropello. The system is that you have a book and the store has one. You write down your order, they copy it in their book and you pay when you wish. At the end of the year you get a percentage back. Signora Bottini heard and approved of my decision and insisted on walking over with me and introducing me to the couple who ran the store. She herself had Giovanni to shop for her, but this was typical of the charming and gracious way that she looked after us.

She not only had a servant, she had three. Two of them had served her lovingly for over forty years. Maria came "by the day" as a general servant and Giannina and Giovanni lived in the gatehouse down on the main road. Whichever one was handy opened the impressive wrought iron gates for the family or guests. Giannina helped up at the villa, and had a touch of magic in raising the chickens and turkeys. Giovanni took care of the grounds, the vegetable garden, their fruit trees and the three cows. When there was ripe fruit or vegetables, he climbed up the long flight of stone steps to the villa just before noon with baskets brimming to overflowing. There were no half measures with him. When he came back down, he had the shopping book for the cooperativo. The noon church bells always found him bicycling over to Gropello. After he handed in his book, and while his order and the Bottini's were being made up, he joined friends for a drink in the bar.

Men with more leisure played "Scopa," a card game, in the bar, or "Botte," a type of bowls, just outside the store. The roof of the porch was still purple with wisteria when I started shopping there in early July.

On his shopping expeditions, Giovanni took time only for a drink and a few jests, for there was always laughter when he passed by. He met Kim and me with his heart in his hand and a warm smile. Lucky indeed were we to bask in the warmth of his friendship.

Getting to know Giannina was slower, but oh, so sweet. Giovanni quickly caught on to our "Hi there" wave. I would come out of my kitchen door onto the balcony and he would be climbing his outside barn steps, and our greetings were pure North American. Giannina had a deep innate dignity that never allowed her to wave, but her heart was as warm as her husband's. If she ever sensed homesickness on my part, her arms were quick to go around me. We made a strange pair at such times, for she fitted under my arm.

Trips to their kitchen became a part of my daily life. I went up in the morning for milk from the morning milking. Noontime would see me making another trip as a baker with a small truck arrangement on a motorcycle came by with crusty rolls and bread. I always shared a roll with "Brill" or "Fritz," the black and white terrier who was chained to guard the barn. The Bottinis called him Brill and Giovanni called him Fritz, and he and I had become good friends. His love of bread was pure Italian. Mother did not care for the crusty bread, and I had found in Varese a type more like American bread, called "Yankee." Once, coming home from a shopping trip, it was the only bread I had, and I gave him a bit of the sliced bread. He left it in the fence corner, and for the first and only time gave me a look of reproach.

At noontime I had to watch for a chance to cross the road because it was alive with bicycle riders going home for their *colazione*, or noonday meal; really, a second colazione, as their breakfast is their *prima colazione*. These were the factory workers from our local factories: furniture, leather goods and pipes. The latter made some pipes for Dunhill. Sad to say, there was also a factory that reclaimed rubber, and the smell from it was sometimes almost unbearable.

These factories not only employed all the adults not busy on farms and in homes but caught all the children not going on to high school. In those days all the children were supposed to go to school until they were fourteen. Primary school was over for them when they were eleven. There was a fee for high school and also transportation costs. If they did not have the financial means to meet this expense, they started an apprenticeship in these local factories.

As I watched all the men, women and young people going home for the noon meal, I felt it was no wonder their home ties were so close, for they spent so much time together. Even the people who worked in Varese came home on the bus to eat with the family. They had higher-paid jobs, and did not have to be back until three. Our local factories allowed only one hour. Gianfranco, the seventeen-year-old son of Giovanni, worked at the furniture factory, and his meal was waiting on the table at twelve. His parents ate later. For the *colazione*, the *contadini* (farmers) would have a pasta dish of noodles, rice, or macaroni, a small amount of meat, a vegetable, green salad, fresh fruit, cheese and wine. Tea, coffee and meat were so expensive that they were usually a weekend treat, and meat was used very sparingly. I knew of one farmer who gave his wife veal chops for her birthday, and she was thrilled.

Supper for the *contadini* in our region was always a huge bowl of soup. This would be thick with fresh, finely chopped vegetables. Then there would be fresh fruit, cheese, wine and bread. All Italians, rich and poor alike, ate bread with every meal.

On the really hot days, I never went into Varese unless absolutely necessary. A breeze from the lake usually cooled things off a bit before 5:00, and I would walk over to Gropello for essentials. My white handkerchief tied to a fence was the signal for Kim to stop for me. Once home, we would be into our bathing suits and out onto our blessed lake. Instead of a boat, we each had rubber mattresses and spent many pleasant hours drifting on them and gazing at the mountains and the picturesque fishing boats. These boats were shaped at the bow like the crescent of a new moon and had an oriental beauty. The men rowed standing and there were times when they would quietly row out of the early morning mist when my breath would catch with the beauty of it all.

It is the custom in Italy to eat late. Stores open after the siesta any time from 3:00 to 4:30 and do not close until 7:30. The hour for dinner varies. When I saw the sun set, I would swim in behind my mattress to start supper. Our sunset in summer did not mean the end of daylight, for it was an unusual one. Suddenly, up in the sky, far from the horizon, the sun would be gone. It set behind Monte Rosa, our highest peak in the Alps. Often, just as it was sliding down behind the mountain, all the surrounding peaks would appear, for a moment or two, outlined in gold.

We ate all the meals we could on the balcony. Kim had to be to work by 8:00, so 7:00 found us breakfasting in the sunshine on our own private balcony off our bedroom. Upstairs, the only window was in the bathroom. All the others were French doors opening onto the balcony; and they were always open, as we lived out there. At noon, the sun was so hot that Mother and I sought a shady spot, but evening would find us dining right in the middle of our front balcony, where we could enjoy to the full the beauty of the lake.

One fisherman, Antonio, must have enjoyed the sight of our table and candle light, for almost every evening he, so dark and strong, and his crescent boat were part of the picture. Somewhere there is a man who has a picture of us dining on our balcony. He had rented a boat and a guide, and was busy with his camera. Our dining on the balcony of our attractive villa appealed to him, and as he went to snap his picture, we three lifted our wine glasses in salute.

To Italy, With Love

Chapter 5

Life at the Lake

It was wonderful to realize that we had two whole years and could take sightseeing at a leisurely pace, and could return again to favourite places. Our first summer we tried many restaurants, some built out over the water at Lago Maggiore, where we could look down and watch the fish swimming gracefully, then look up to the mountains; and other restaurants tucked away in gardens where we ate under the trees. The more we ate out, the more the waiters impressed me. They worked quickly and with real pleasure in their work. There was vigour and a gusto that made you feel they were proud of their profession. Many were short, this being a way of earning a living where lack of height is an asset, being easier on the back. Some of the waiters put so much agility into serving, it became almost a ballet. One of Mother's treasured memories was the time she ordered a banana and the head waiter peeled it with a knife and fork, sliced it and arranged it in a perfect circle with a grace and flair that lifted the operation into artistry.

The wine in Italy was one of our great delights. Mother quickly settled for the golden Orvieto, but Kim and I savoured and tried wines until the day we left Italy. If we had been satisfied with a certain local wine, we could have it very cheaply, for the deposit on the bottle was often more than the price of the wine. Every district has its own wine and its own cheeses, as well as regional dishes. We did not want to miss anything and had some real gastronomic experiences.

We never paid a bill without thoroughly checking every item. You are respected for this. I know many feel they are cheated in Italy. I had fallen so completely in love with Italy and the Italians that I was always trying to figure out why they did certain things. I was almost like a doting mother making allowances and excuses. I decided that if you pay your bill without checking it, it looks as if you have no regard for money. Here the realistic mind of the Italian steps in. If you have so much that you can be casual about it, then maybe they, or he, can have some of it. It is worth a try anyway. They do not have the respect for law and private property that some have. In their history of siege and conquest, the laws were not made with their interests at heart, but were made to make life better and richer for the winner of the time. This state of affairs made them turn in on themselves. They developed a patience and a cheerfulness that carried them through difficult times. It was this that gave them their capacity for living and taking pleasure in life. This and their family was all they could count on. People tend to forget that Italy has been unified for only a little over a hundred years. It is often difficult for people who have been part of a nation for centuries to make allowances for a younger nation. It is difficult also for people who have had laws they could respect to understand people who had found that to the quick-witted fell the spoils.

I could understand the reasoning that made people of the north evade paying income tax if they could, since as yet they saw no reason why any of the money they worked so hard for should go to help the south. The good of the laws had yet to be proven to many of them. I felt I understood much of what they did, but one thing I could never understand was how they could use a lovely lake as a garbage dump. I had to be constantly on the alert. When our kitchen shelves and cupboards arrived after a few weeks of making do with a few boxes and a plank, I caught the driver just as he was dumping all the cardboard and packing into the lake.

Our two plum trees produced a crop much appreciated by the fruit-loving Italians. Guests would sit on our balcony and shoot the pits over with never a thought for our lawn. Twice, I had spent a good part of a day collecting tins, roots, etc. from the lake bottom and was waiting for Kim's help to move it away, only to have a guest push it all back in. When I asked why, when they obviously appreciated beauty, I was told that Italians lived for the moment. I knew this and also felt I knew how it had come about, but I found it impossible to understand their lack of foresight. Whatever was put in the lake in front of our place was going to be there for us to look at and swim through or around. It fell to Kim and me to guard our lakefront. We had to accept this as we had to accept the fishermen.

The enthusiasm for fishing was one of my Italian surprises. I was even more surprised to learn that our lake had been fished for thousands of years. Almost two thousand years before the birth of Christ, lake-dwellers lived in small villages built on piles in the lake. The excavation site of early lake-dwellers, not far from the villa on the island, was one of the local sights I could show our visitors. I would rent a boat at Gropello and row them over to the island. Later, I would take them into the museum in Varese where they could study all the finds that had been made.

These early lake-dwellers used hooks of bone and nets of bark fibre. While we lived on the lake, thirty-three professional fishermen, mostly living in Calcinate del Pesce and countless devoted amateurs fished the lake ceaselessly. The amateurs trolled with hand lines from rented boats on the weekends. Fortunately these boats were rowboats or quiet motor boats. The professionals used nets, every day but Sunday. The nets were set about little bays in the lake, or in front of reed beds and the fish were driven into them by whacking the surface of the water with a long board. The noise was deafening above water, and under water must have driven the fish nearly to distraction.

We first heard the noise about 4:00 a.m. one morning soon after we moved in, and spent an irate fifteen minutes finding out what it was. We always warned guests about it, but the noise took some getting used to.

The amazing fact was that after being fished steadily, the lake was still full of fish. At times it was literally hopping with them. They were mostly perch and not very large. A quarter pound was a special prize, though we once had a giant of at least two pounds, washed up on the shore. The lake is only about nine kilometers long and four wide at the widest point.

This fecundity of the lake is in keeping with the general fruit-fulness of the region. Everything grows like mad. When we moved in at the end of June, there had already been two crops of hay taken off the fields, and there were to be two more before the winter.

We cut all the branches off the plane trees in front of the house about the first of July to give more air and a better view. By the middle of August the trees had new crowns.They were twigs, not more than about three-eighths of an inch in diameter, but the growth was phenomenal. For someone coming from our short Deep River season, it was breathtaking.

Quite breathtaking also was the supply of fruit and vegetables Giovanni brought to us. Signor Bottini had told him to share with us whenever there was an abundance. There must have been a frequent abundance, for there would so often be a clear, ringing "Signora, Signora," and I would hurry to the kitchen side of the balcony. There would be Giovanni with brimming baskets and a beaming smile. How a man in his early sixties could contrive to have the smile of a boy I will never know, but he managed it. Even his hair had a boyish, tousled look. We would meet down in the cool of the ground floor level under our front balcony. It was floored with small stones set in cement, a clever feature of Italian paving. I will never forget the fruit and vegetables I received down there. I kept telling him to bring me less, but it never did any good. On those days – and I never knew when they would be – I could have run a small restaurant.

Our place was a bower of flowers as well, both from the Bottini's formal garden and from Giannina's own private gar-den. To save Giannina the walk all the way down the lane, I gave her a bell. When I heard it, she and I would meet up by the fence. It might be flowers, a message from Signora Bottini, a phone message, and sometimes it would be freshly churned butter.

Silvia, of the Hotel Europa, introduced us to life in the country and gave us an afternoon to remember. She got word to us that her cherry tree was ripe, and that she would like to share cherries with us. We called for her and another maid from the Europa, Angela, at 2:00 o'clock one Saturday afternoon. We drove out into the country, and wound our way up the hillside on the far shore of our lake until, high on the hilltop, we came to the village of Brunello. Then we walked slowly with Silvia down a narrow cobbled lane, meeting her daughter-in-law who worked in the village *tabaccaio*. We turned in through an arched doorway in a wooden wall, silvered with age, and looked up into the beams and hay of an ancient barn. Silvia's home away from the hotel was as neat and compact as could be, just a room in a series of small apartments built right into the barnyard.

We met elderly relatives who were quietly and slowly washing clothes in outside tubs in the sunshine, and others preparing fresh vegetables for the thick evening soup. We had a drink of wine. Something must be served. It is part of the rite of Italian hospitality.

Then we set off for the cherry tree with a dear old uncle of eighty-five. It was a glorious summer day with a breeze blowing, and high up there on the hilltop. The world seemed to be ours alone. We walked along the country road enjoying the wild flowers and watching the lizards darting about. It was peaceful beyond belief. We passed a church enclosure that was considered sanctified ground, as once in July snow had fallen there. The wonder of this had led to the blessing of the spot.

The cherry tree turned out to be a beauty, over twenty feet in height, standing alone in their field. The field must have been over a half mile from the barn. As I looked at the one lone tree, I wondered if someone long ago had dropped a pit from a picnic lunch, for why would the one tree be away off here by itself?

The tiny, old uncle made his way over to a stone hut that had the usual tiled roof, and produced an ancient, but reliable, ladder. All bits of farmland have these attractive old stone buildings where farm equipment is stored. From the first minute I saw them, I was always imagining them as little homes. I know of one of the larger ones, on the way to Gavirate, that has been made into a charming retreat.

With the ladder against the tree, we five were soon settled up there eating the irresistible cherries and filling our baskets. Just as a sudden rain will sometimes bring people closer together, so our time up in the branches of that tree produced a close, warm, friendly relationship. It was such a lovely afternoon. Angela was young and brimming over with life, and she made such a contrast to the bent old uncle, who was remarkably agile but careful to conserve his energy.

We delivered Silvia and Angela back to the hotel, and saw the beaming pleasure on the faces of the Stabilinis when they saw the velvety, black cherries Silvia had brought to them. To have had that afternoon up on the quiet hilltop, to have seen how a whole family lived in what I had thought was just a huge barn, made me realize anew how lucky we were to have the time to get to know Italy so unhurriedly.

Often on Saturdays, Kim just had to drive us to see things he had discovered on his trips to and from work. He had found two treasures of washing places. One was quite lyrically beautiful, a curved stone trough fed by a small spring, and only big enough for one washer. Another was a large one off in a field under a single, magnificent tree. He also showed us a handsome Spanish villa built in the fourteenth century, at a time when the Spanish had waged war right down the road from our house.

Kim had to show us the railroad barrier that had caused the first damage to our new car. The very first day Kim drove the car to work, he arrived at a railway crossing just as the barrier on the far side of the track lowered. Within a second, the near barrier crashed down with a thud on our car roof. It had been hiding between two buildings. To Kim's horror, adventurous Vespa riders kept sneaking under the near barrier, crossing the track and darting under the far barrier. To avoid a disaster, Kim felt he had to back up to let the barrier down to its rightful position. There was a sickening sound as the rail rasped over the surface of our shiny new car.

At the end of this first day of driving, Kim could scarcely write his name. He had lost control of his shaking hand. There had been too many unusual things to contend with on the country roads.

We soon found it was a race to cross railroad crossings in the country before the barriers came down. One railroad attendant could be working two crossings. He bicycled from one crossing to another. This could result in a long wait, as he seemed to bicycle slowly in a ruminating, philosophical, way. Allowing for this leisurely process, one man lost his goat. He tied it to a conveniently lowered barrier and slipped into a *tabaccaio* for a drink. As is the way with Italians and conversation, he lost track of time, and when he looked out, the barrier had been raised and his poor goat had been hanged.

While the custodian of the railway barriers may be a leisurely cyclist, bicycle racers are quite another breed. We met up with our first bicycle race on a Sunday, when we were out to explore the neighbouring city of Como and to visit its fine old cathedral. It had been a peaceful drive through pastoral country in warm sunshine when, suddenly, an agitated and excited group waved us to the side of the road. Soon wave after wave of bicycle riders, pedaling at an incredible speed, went whizzing past. Then came the interested followers in cars and on Vespas. Never run your time schedule too fine in Italy when driving, for anything, from a bicycle race to a local festival to a market, can hold you up.

A town or city usually has its market square, and there are always a certain number of stalls doing business. Those that sell fruit and vegetables can be certain of daily trade. The rest of the market space is used for parking when there is no scheduled market. On regular market days every bit of space has someone selling something. Every town has a market day, and then the main street may be closed to traffic, and you have to find some other way through the town.

Early in the morning, trucks, carriers contrived out of Vespas, carts, barrows and automobiles arrive in town, and wares are spread out everywhere. Even sidewalk space is taken up. There can be some tricky traffic snarls as many leave their vehicles just where it suits them with not a thought for future traffic. By 8:00

a.m. the market is in full swing, and it is as gay and colourful as a fair.

The markets were such a delight to me that I had to arrive just once early enough to watch the whole show. The first thing unpacked is the canvas for the walls and the awnings of the stalls. Then an incredible assortment and amount of articles appear. For me there was an element of pure magic in these unpackings. How they packed so much into the little vans amazed me.

I have always been attracted to donkeys. Bobbiate, a village on our way to Varese, went in for donkeys for some reason. On market days, I had the pleasure of watching their dainty feet as they pulled their two-wheeled cart of vegetables into the market. I found their forward pull and the rhythmical twitching of their ears very soothing. Somehow it seemed to me that they had a more philosophical expression on the homeward trip. The markets carried Kim back to Peking days. It was the awnings, the colour and the quality and type of the homemade articles, especially those made of wood.

Gavirate was our nearest town to have a market. Kim would drop me off there on a Thursday morning about 7:45 as it was on his way to work. My steps would always quicken as I approached the market. My shopping bags, made of green plastic string, would swing loosely at my sides; and I would warn myself that they must not get too full, that I must get on a bus later and then get down our lane with them. My warnings never seemed to do much good. The spirit of the market went to my head and my bags bulged so that I could hardly carry them. Frequently, I had to leave one in Giannina's kitchen and return for it.

There were booths for cheese, fish, olive oil, wine, shoes, woollens, anything you could possibly want that could be transported easily. The banter and talk was as gay as the scene itself. I found hairpins such as I had given up all hope of ever finding. The dear old soul who had that tiny booth did everything but put them in my hair for me, she was so delighted in my pleasure at finding them. The older people generally had smaller stalls; the really old might have no more than a basket of lemons. Italians use so many lemons they could be sure of an empty basket when the market was over.

For a while, I felt a twinge of guilt on market day in Gavirate. I soon discovered that prices in this town were lower than in Varese; so for general shopping I made it a habit to leave with Kim, stop off in Gavirate to shop, and then catch the 9:00 bus home. On market days, as I struggled past my usual stores with my bulging bags, my conscience bothered me. The kindly store people never seemed to hold it against me nor to resent the market produce that overflowed onto the sidewalk practically to their doors.

The bus on the homeward trip carried more than a bit of the market spirit. There was always chatter and joking among the passengers, but on market days it was particularly cheerful. Everyone was helping everyone else with their purchases. I would look at the happy faces, many of them fine old faces, others young and without much character as yet, and I rejoiced in their pleasure. At such times I often thought, sadly, of the many strained and unhappy faces that I had seen on the streets of New York. There was a dignity, a character and a strength in the faces of so many of the peasants that was often lacking in the faces of the wealthier. Somehow, market days always brought this home to me.

Often times I arranged it so that I could be at the market at closing time, for I was fascinated by the folding and packing away process. In the morning, they seemed to love driving up with their wares and spreading them out. After a friendly day with the public, and each other, there was no sadness in the storing away of things not sold. Somehow, you could already feel the excitement of the next day's market.

There were gypsies in our part of Italy. Whenever they moved into our neighbourhood, there was a feeling of great unease among the Italians. Gypsies are so quiet and so self-contained, and are such a law unto themselves. They are slim and small-boned, and have impenetrable brown eyes. They look hard at you, but somehow you could never see into their eyes. There was a great air of mystery about them, and you had a feeling of fear. The women wore long, loose, swinging skirts. What the men did I never knew, but the women and children were the most persistent beggars. They never spoke. It was just that brown cupped hand held up in front of you. Kim had a magic way of getting rid of them. He would say in rapid Italian: "I work for my money, why don't you?" They just melted away at that. I had no magic formula and they plagued me. When I took guests to the La Scala opera museum and opera house, I had to steel myself, for they had a regular beat there. Thank goodness they came to Varese only occasionally. They would camp out in the country for a few days, and the women and children would beg the streets in the city. There was a great feeling of relief when they moved on. The only laughter I ever heard from them was once in Varese when I had a little change and was feeling weak. First one begged from me and then another. I had given more to a small boy than to a young woman and he was gloating over his higher take, and they were both laughing happily.

During that first summer of exploring the surrounding countryside, there were some places we did not inquire about, preferring to have them remain places of mystery. One was a lovely villa high on the tiered hill behind us. I sometimes waited for the Varese bus with a woman who worked up there, but always resisted the temptation to question her. Another of our mystery places was partway up the mountainside, an old courtyard with buildings of elegance and classic beauty. All was old and deserted, yet there was a spell about the place. There was a feeling of courtly life and of great dignity, as the buildings crumbled and the grounds grew more wild and tangled. Some family had put its mark on that place, for the atmosphere still lingered so strongly that you felt it as soon as you looked through the fine old iron gates.

Our visit, one Sunday, to the estate of Signorina Maria Sala, our friend from the Europa, was a step back into the past. She had finally decided that she had to be practical in spite of her strong attachment to the estate. She had found a buyer and invited us to visit her home before she sold it. We arrived in the piazza of her village before noon, and asked directions of a woman all in black. The smile of pleasure that lit up her fine country face as she pronounced Signorina Maria's name let us know how much Maria was loved and respected. We did not know that the gate we were to watch for was set in a wall, and we drove by, still looking. We realized we had missed the gate when a white-haired man dressed in what I call Dutch blue, came racing up to us on a bicycle. Our guide in black, back on the town square, had walked briskly to the corner to see we had gotten her directions straight. When she saw us drive past the gate, she ran to a shop, explained about us, and our white-haired rescuer must have thrown himself on a bicycle and peddled madly to our rescue. This was typical of the extraordinarily helpfulness we found so often in Italy.

When we were guided back and drove through the gate we had missed, Kim marveled at the similarity to China. So many times during our stay in Italy he would say "Kate, this is just like China." It might be a market place, certain roads or buildings. This time it was the way the large villa and the servants' quarters were built into a compound, walled in as in China. Maria's family had been in the silk business and there was a series of red brick buildings where the silk worms had been housed and where the various processes of the silk industry had taken place. There were no more silk worms, but the mulberry trees were still there.

The villa had twenty-two rooms and had been the family home for over two centuries. Downstairs there were no halls; you passed through one room to the next. During its family history, the wood panelling in the dining room had been carved with the same design as was on the massive sideboard and the handsome chairs. We had a delicious dinner. In her note of invitation, Maria assured us it would be just a simple lunch; she would not fuss. We could not have eaten more, but every bite was delicious. All the fruit and vegetables had come from the garden we had visited earlier.

After our *colazione*, we were allowed to see the huge old kitchen with all its old cooking ranges and fireplace, as well as the more modern appliances.

Then, Maria asked me to come upstairs to see that the room she had prepared for Mother's siesta was suitable. As in China, there is great respect in Italy for the older person. When we climbed the narrow flight of stone steps, I had one of my many surprises in Italy. At the top of the stairs was an ornate, but very strong, iron gate reaching to the ceiling, with an iron railing of the same height running along the hallway. In earlier times, when the family retired, they were safe from possible surprise attack once this gate was locked. This iron work, and a huge marble bath tub like I had seen in museums, were from the past and were too solid to be moved. A spring kept a tap running continuously. This running tap I had seen in older Italian houses. Giannina had one in her humble home.

I found Maria's concern that Mother's room should be just right very touching. After all Mother had eaten and had seen, she could have fallen asleep sitting bolt upright. Everything she could possibly wish for was handy in the room chosen for her siesta.

We went on down the hall, and I saw Maria's room, which had been her mother and father's. After all these years, she was still conscious of the honour of having a room that had belonged to her parents. The view from the balcony I will never forget. Theirs was a beautiful garden with fine old trees, and when one family has loved and cared for a garden for over two hundred years, it has had time to grow very beautiful. It was truly more a park. Kim and I explored it while Mother and Maria had their siestas. We found little arbors where the family had enjoyed tea. We sat on benches under the great old trees and absorbed the quiet beauty, shut off from the rest of the world by old stone walls.

The church bell in the village kept reminding us that there was an outside world. The church bells in Italy were one of my great delights. Where we lived, they came to us from over the lake, from the mountainside, and from farther down the lakeshore. I always tried to keep Friday afternoons free to sit on our balcony, for from one church across the lake there was such lovely music I hated to miss it. I asked Kim if he had heard anything about the schedule of bell ringing. He suggested that perhaps the rope was left hanging and anyone passing could give the bell a tug.

After the siesta, we had tea in the garden. Tea was another surprise for me. I had not realized that it was so much a part of Italian life, but all the families I met had afternoon tea. After tea, we went through a few more of the downstairs rooms. When I saw all the family possessions that one small woman had to part with, I could understood the anguish she had experienced when we were at the Europa. For example, there had been a charming young cousin that the family all loved. He had decided to go to South America to make his fortune, and came to Maria to say his goodbyes before setting sail from Genoa. In two days, he was back to tell my friend that he loved her. While she loved him dearly, she had not thought of him as a husband, and so he left for South America. After six weeks in his new home, he died of fever. All his belongings, even his brush and comb, were sent back to Maria. His two saddles, all adorned with silver, were still in one of the rooms. In another room there hung a painting of him.

The walls of the house were all hung with paintings, many of them of the family. The enormity of the task ahead of poor Maria quite overwhelmed me. The whole place breathed atmosphere, and if we could feel it so strongly, how much stronger it must have been for her. It was hard that Sunday to say goodbye to Maria and to her home. She had an apartment in Milan and another in Varese, where she had gathered her most treasured possessions. She had a servant in her Milanese home but looked after herself in Varese. Having seen her family home, and the size of it, I could appreciate her delight when she told me how exciting it was to be able to get up in the night and make herself a cup of tea.

While there was great delight in my new life, I had my problems too. The language was my greatest problem. I worked daily, writing out vocabularies and getting Mother to hear me rehearse at lunchtime. I made many mistakes but I had no feeling of inferiority. There was lots of laughter and fun. We laughed together, not they at me. One day shopping, I wanted celery (*sedano*) and instead asked for *cedro*, a cedar tree. Of course it was too good a chance for my storekeeper to let pass. Was it just a little tree I wanted, or was it something in the nature of forty feet? The forty feet had me really puzzled, until I realized my mistake. In my eagerness to talk and my pleasure in my newly gained words, I would forget all about the necessity of masculine and feminine endings. Kim kept at me to remember the rule of "Oh boy, and Ah girl," which helped.

Then there were dialects to contend with, and being in the country meant that dialects were much in use. Calcinate and Gropello were just a mile apart, yet some of their dialect words were quite different. To make my problem even harder, Giannina came from Calcinate and Giovanni from Gropello. When I would finally get a little dialect down pat, I would distress Signora Bottini. Dialect was not spoken in polite company.

Kim's quick ear picked up the different words, and he delighted the local people by being able to use their special words. Giovanni would be so pleased he just had to throw an arm around Kim's shoulder and give him a hug. Much or most of it was pure puzzlement for me. I was striving for a working vocabulary, not concerned with grammar. That was problem enough for me without trying to cope with the *dialetto*.

But I was not the only one having language problems. We were invited to a very beautiful home in Varese. Mother could not understand the conversation in Italian, but she was enjoying the elegance of the home. Suddenly our host said in halting English "Woulda you helpa me witha my English lesson?" He got out his book and started "A newsapaper is composed of a number of shits of paper." Now, this Mother could understand, and she was having great difficulty controlling herself. He never was able to pronounce sheets. Finally, Kim said "Well you may have something there."

I realized how difficult English is as a language when an Italian lady asked me if she was saying "Shao Bowat" correctly. I felt I deserved a prize when I realized she was trying to say "Show Boat."

Kim would occasionally bring home someone visiting the Centre at Ispra. I remember one chap coming down from Brussels. First we swam until the sun set and then we had dinner on our balcony by candlelight and listened to Chopin records, with a three-quarter moon making a path of gold on the quiet lake. Brussels is a beautiful city, but he had left it cold and rainy. The magic of that Italian night had him longing to share the beauty of it all with his wife.

Whenever the moon was full, I saw to it that we shared the beauty with guests and friends. We often had people to dinner, or to our balcony in the evening to try Canadian cakes and cookies and enjoy our lake by moonlight. One evening two of the Italian chaps Kim worked with and their wives, and the two-year old son of one couple, came for the evening. I was amazed to find that although the men had been working together for four months, this was the first time the wives had met. They were both eager for company and yet, because of the formalities of Italian society, they had never met. In the four months she had been in Varese, one of the wives had not met anyone from Ispra.

We were also amazed that no functions were organized where people could get to know each other after working hours. We carried on as we always had in Canada, entertaining people and striving to let them taste Canadian dishes. Waffles and maple syrup were a great favourite. I had anticipated this, so I took my waffle iron and plugged it in to our Italian transformer. When Angelo had waffles for the first time, Kim did not notice that my supply was finished and said to him, "Have you had enough?" and Angelo's immediate answer was "There aren't any more, are there?"

Reinier, our Dutch friend, was such a whole-hearted fan of maple syrup that his wife, Bimbi, said she was almost jealous of the stuff.

These gatherings of mixed nationalities were most interesting for me. I found the Dutch most like us in their spirit and enthusiasm. The Germans share our great love of the outdoors. I think our summer cottage living and camping, and washing at the lake's edge, would be quite incomprehensible to many Italians. They expect certain refinements in their way of living and they get them. I will never forget my surprise in finding that after skiing all day high in the mountains, we could come into a delicious meal, all five courses being served. Lo and behold, there would be the veal, complete with a slice of lemon and a curl of anchovy, and all this high on a mountain top.

Occasionally, in our evenings of mixed nationalities, there were some tense moments. One evening we had a Dutch couple and a German couple, the husbands both senior scientists, and somehow we got onto the subject of the last war. It just happened the region the Dutch came from had been none too happy under the Germans. I realized we would have to be very careful where we let the conversation wander. Once we heard a German express great surprise that the Italians had been down on him for wearing shorts in Milan. This was soon after the war and he had not realized that his dress proclaimed his nationality and that Germans were not popular in many parts of Italy.

Many of the Germans and the Dutch spoke very good Italian. The French, not so good. The Germans and the Dutch that we knew had so entered into the spirit of the country and the language that they had acquired much of the hand language as well. Italian is a very beautiful language, but it is not so rich in shades of meaning. The Italians, with their graceful hands, have made up for this lack of verbal expression. They have developed a language of the hands that enriches their spoken language, and is a delight to watch.

When an Italian wants to interrupt, one sure way of achieving his purpose is to hold the hands of the person who is talking. I knew I was becoming more fluent the first time this happened to me. Kim and I started learning this hand language from Silvia as soon as we moved into the Europa. What delighted me was to see Germans carry Italian hand language into their own language. You could hear them saying "nein, nein" with the finger movement the Italians always used for "no." There is also a way the Italians hit the right elbow with the left hand to mean a person has made an escape.

In this sign language, to hold up your index finger and your little finger with the others doubled into a fist is the sign of the *cornuto*, literally, "horned." This is the sign for a cuckold, as a cuckold is supposed to wear horns invisibly on his head. It is the Italian driver's way of swearing at you, just letting you know what he thinks of you as a driver. We were driving along when I saw this sign for the first time. I explained the sign to Kim and told him the man we had just passed had made this sign at us. Kim said "Oh, he did, did he?" Such a wild look came over his face that I expected to see horns on him. Later, I was told with a soft chuckle that you can make this cornuto sign to a northerner's face, but the southern temperament being as it is, you are advised to make the sign behind a southerner's back.

As well as learning the sign language, we learned that raised voices with Italians does not necessarily mean anger. I was quite horrified and saddened one day when I went for my milk to hear Giannina and Giovanni roaring at each other. I thought it must be a fight, but there was laughter in their eyes. Their place had been painted and they were just rearranging the furniture and thoroughly enjoying themselves.

I bought my milk from Giovanni even though it was not pasteurized because it was difficult to beat the Italian way of life. I had gone to a little dairy in Varese where they sold pasteurized milk and saw, out the back, the family happily pouring the pasteurized milk into bottles they had been washing under running water from a tap. I thought "So much for pasteurisation!" I looked at Giovanni's cows. They were fine looking animals. They were T.B. tested and everyone in the district who drank their milk looked healthy, so I joined the local ranks. My morning walk up the lane to Giannina's kitchen became a part of my daily life and enriched my life from the point of view of language and human kindness. Depending on when I arrived, I might find them having their breakfast of bread soaked in milk; or Giannina might be putting lunch on to simmer while she went up to clean the upstairs of the Bottini's villa. She made the best slow-simmering stew I have ever tasted. They often coaxed me to stay for lunch when I made my noon trip to get bread from the little motorcycle truck that roared up. A few times when Mother was sleeping due to a bad cold, I joined them for lunch. Gianfranco had to eat rapidly to get back to the furniture factory, but we three would linger over the meal, with Giannina's favourite cat Trotti purring away by the wood stove.

While some health regulations seemed so lax, I was impressed by how good the T.B. check on the cows was. I found also that there was a very strict check on the selling of dead animals. In discussing this, a German friend of ours said "Yes, the strict enforcement of that law is very hard on my brother-in-law's lions." I was getting used to surprises in Italy, but this really jolted me. It appeared that her brother-in-law, who lived in the country near Bologna, just fancied keeping lions and was allowed in Italy to do so.

That first summer was a time of wonder and learning for me.

To Italy, With Love

Chapter 6

Visitors and Visits

Our mail arrived any time between 11:00 and 12:30, and was brought by our *portalettera*, a rather handsome young man with a most pleasant smile and friendly disposition. His disposition was most important to Mother, as often for days on end his friendly *"Buon Giorno"* was the only conversation Mother had with anyone other than Kim and me. His name was Franco, and he made his trip out from Varese on a motorbike, weather permitting. When he considered the roads too icy, he would bicycle out. For us, Franco's call was one of the big events of our lives, both for his company, brief as it often was, and when we received letters from home.

One day towards the end of that first summer, he handed me a letter that just transported me. It was from Mary, my second oldest sister. I am lucky enough to have grown up with four sisters and a brother. I sat down on the bottom step of our stairs to read it in the sunshine. Soon, I was pelting up our stairs to give

Mother the news. Mary and her husband Gordon were coming to Europe on business and would come to see us.

We knew what day they were to arrive but not what train, so I decided to meet all the afternoon trains. I was so excited that I read the bus timetable incorrectly. I got up to the bus stop to discover the bus I wanted went only on holidays. Giannina, on her way to feed the chickens and turkeys, told me of my mistake. Giovanni, working in the barn, joined us; and as so often happens in Italy when any crisis turns up, a crowd quickly gathered. This time it was a small group of men doing some roadwork. They all wore jaunty straw hats with a bright band proclaiming their occupation. The situation was explained to them and they became just as excited and just as worried as I was about my delay in getting to the station. Their foreman took charge and flagged down the first car that came along. An earnest conversation ensued. The driver of the car was told of my plight: a sister and her husband were arriving from Canada on their first visit to "La Bell' Italia" and I might be late to meet them. There was a quick smile of understanding from the driver, and as I climbed in beside him, it seemed the whole group was talking at once. The straw hats were waved enthusiastically as we drove off.

My driver friend had carried on a rapid fire conversation all the way to the station. Thank goodness not many answers were demanded of me, for by now my excitement was such that I could not have been coherent in English, let alone in my limited Italian. However, my thanks were convincing enough as I made my way into the Stazione Nord. I hunted up the station master and explained that it was necessary for me to meet all afternoon trains coming into his station and also the Stazione Statale, the other, nearby station. "Please, please, in case my sister arrives when I am over at the other station, could I put up a sign?" Well, it had never been done before, but in this case since it was her first visit to Italy, yes. So I made my two signs: "Mary, wait, I am meeting trains at other station," and I started meeting trains.

It turned out that Mary and Gordon had arrived on a much earlier train with no Italian money and no Italian language. Switzerland makes it so easy for the traveller that, like many others, they had been lulled into a false sense of security. In Switzerland, any type of money was accepted and their best French was answered in perfect English. In Varese it had to be Italian and Italian money. With the aid of their Latin, they managed to check their bags, but had to walk the streets from 12:30 until 3:00, as all the banks were closed for the noon meal and siesta. When they had money, the dining rooms were closed. Fortunately, they thought of the Albergo Europa, where two of the Stabilinis spoke English. As a special favour to us they were given lunch in the cool dining room.

The Stabilinis phoned Kim, for Mary realized that with no Italian, a taxi might easily present yet another problem. Late in the afternoon the three of them found me, still meeting trains in a high state of excitement. What a reunion it was! Happy as I was, I remembered to collect the signs and present my long-awaited sister to the, by now, really interested station master. The road workers waved even more enthusiastically on my return trip. The group was much farther along the road and they must have been watching for me. I had to explain the joyously exuberant greeting to a delighted but somewhat puzzled Mary, Gordon and Kim.

What did they want to see and what did they want to do? What they wanted most of all was to see the type of life we lived. After their delight in our compact, attractive pagoda villa and in the beauty of our lake, we walked them up the lane. With a beaming Giovanni and a dignified, but wiggling, Fritz we showed them the barn. They climbed the outside stairway on the south side where hay, wood and fruit were stored. I pointed out the clothes lines along the little balcony that could make good use of all the southern exposure but had protection against a sudden shower. They, as have so many others, fell in love with the open brick barn windows. Bricks are used in the windows in attractive patterns to let in the air, and yet to give more strength to the building.

Next, we walked them up the lane past the persimmon trees, with the stream on one side and the fruit trees on the other side. They saw how the grapes grew on wires, fixed to these trees. During the daytime, the turkeys and chickens spent time there and made good use of any fruit that fell. As we crossed the main road, they had to stop to enjoy the beauty of the ironwork of the Bottini's gate. Then, the smiling face of Giannina greeted them from the kitchen door.

Everything within the Bottini's property interested them: the laurel tree where I had been told to pick my own fresh bay leaves, the great cedars of Lebanon, and, especially, the dwarf cyclamen growing among the rocks in the garden by the steps leading up to the villa.

No conversation of words was possible between them and the Bottinis, but there is a language of the eyes and the smiles. And oh, how graciously they were received! We all had a drink of ice cold vermouth with a shaving of lemon peel. Each drink was served on its own small silver tray and lace doily. Hospitality is all important in an Italian household, and there is a graciousness and formality about it that I find enchanting. I could tell Mary and Gordon were delighted to be seeing how a well-to-do family lived in the country. They saw the patio that was the roof of the three-car garage, and how the trees had been allowed to grow up through this roof to give shade by day and to give that mysterious something that trees give off. Italians love to eat under trees. They saw the fountain trickling over the rocks where fresh flowers were always placed in tribute to the lovely statue of theVirgin Mary. They were pleased also with the huge round dining room table out under the plane trees. They also saw the large formal dining room in the house, and the small, intimate dining room just off the kitchen. I pointed out that, since eating is such a joy in Italy, the dining room is often a much larger room than the living room.

We were able to share with Mary and Gordon the evening show of the moving of the fowl across the road. Once, years before, the chickens had been stolen from the barnyard, and ever since, they had spent the nights in close to Giovanni. If there was a dog at the time of the theft, he could not have been of the same calibre as Fritz. Giovanni would scare the chickens into crates and load them onto a large wheelbarrow, wheel them across the road and release them in the enclosure behind his house. This in itself could be fun to watch, for the chickens tried hard to preserve a certain dignity throughout this rather undignified proceeding.

Next came the turkeys, and it was a fight between Giovanni's boisterous nature and the dignified treatment they felt was their due. While his technique was one of brute force, a whack here and a dart there, Giannina had a way that was pure magic. She loved her birds and they loved her. She could have lured them anywhere with her voice. That evening the show was as usual. Giovanni had them all ready by the small gate. They were stiffly proud and seething with indignation at his treatment of them. There was a lull in the traffic on the roadway, and from the other side of the road, Giannina gave her soft chirping call the turkeys had heard from the time they had hatched. Giovanni opened the gate and those turkeys ran like joyous young children to a beloved mother. All dignity was gone; they were chicks again. Once the crossing was over, they flew up into the trees in the garden to spend the night.

We four were all chuckling about the show as our turn came to cross the road. For dinner that night we went to a restaurant where we could look down from the hillside on the fields sweeping down to our beloved lake. Kim and I were delighted, for already they seemed to be enjoying Italy the way we did. At first, I was all for cooking for them and then I thought, no, one of the great joys of Italy is eating, and they must enjoy all of Italy's dishes, not my version of Italian cooking.

That evening was in the season for melons and *prosciutto crudo*. The melons are cut into small crescents and the waiter skillfully severs them from the skin and then heaps your plate with paper thin slices of *proscuitto crudo*, a specially cured ham. Mary liked it so much, it did not take her long to find it when they returned to Toronto. Next we treated them to a *pasta*, a delicious noodle dish, well flavoured with cheese. Then the inevitable veal, the most popular meat in Italy. The *zuccini* were at their best, and they were lightly fried and sprinkled with cheese. When you eat an Italian meal, you do not want a rich dessert, but are perfectly satisfied with salad and fruit. It takes a while to accustom oneself to the strong, potent coffee, so we ordered *cappuccino* for them.

As we sat and talked, the hotel garden, the little farms and orchards, and the lake gradually dimmed into the twilight, and then disappeared into the night. Next morning it was hard for Kim to leave us and drive off to work. At breakfast, I had to explain to Mary that the awful whacking that had wakened them about 4:00 a.m. was the commercial fishermen beating the water to drive the fish into their nets.

Those few days were pure delight for us, to be able to enjoy our beloved Italy with family, and to have family with us again. Mother had a chance to talk with someone other than Kim and me. We drove them here and walked them there, and dined them where they could have lovely views and special dishes. We took them to the Hermitage, a small hotel nearby, with an English garden atmosphere. It was renowned for its *cannellone*. This is a pasta where the meat paste is rolled into a cone of noodle-like dough, and then comes a divine tomato paste, and then the liberal sprinkling of cheese. Like so many hotels and villas in Italy, the Hermitage was not right on the water's edge but up on a hillside, where you could enjoy the view of the whole lake. As well as its cannellone, this hotel was one of the places to eat *pesce persico*, the little perch from our lake. These were fried in just a coating of flour and liberally salted and were delicious. The

Calcinate fishermen kept all our district supplied with this delicacy.

Gordon had only two days with us but left with a good impression of our rural life, how good Italian food could be, and how kind and gracious Italian people are. I was able to take Mary on the Lago Maggiore cruise to Isola Bella. This was my fourth trip and by now I was a capable guide. The official tour of the island was in Italian, French and German, and whenever I was along, I had at least a few English-speaking travellers eagerly listening to what I had managed to glean. Mary and I had a golden day for our trip. On my first visit, I had seen the gardens and villas and the hotels ablaze with the exotic colours of the azaleas and rhododendron. This time the hydrangeas were great fountains of colour. The tour of gardens of the palace was of great interest to Mary as she is a keen gardener.

On our short stop in Stresa, between boats I realized how thrilled Mary was with our favourite shop there. Kim met us as we landed in Laveno. I took him aside, and asked if we could pick Mother up and drive to Stresa for dinner, so that Mary could have a real shopping spree. The glow in her eyes at the thought of more time in that fabulous shop made Kim count the drive as nothing. This special shop has all the things Italian that one would like to take home to loved ones. As she shopped for her family, every so often she would say, "Kate, if later on I send you the money, would you buy this for me?" One thing she could not resist for herself were some exquisitely carved, tiny, gilt angels. She was already working them into her Christmas decorations. Mother, who could never resist shops, bought herself a lovely evening bag of soft white leather, all decorated with gold.

Mary left us to rejoin Gordon in Switzerland for their homeward trip. Her visit was perfect in every respect, except that Monte Rosa and the other mountains never once appeared during the five days she was with us. From then on our *Porta Lettera* was interested to know which of my Canadian letters was from *la sua sorella Maria*.

One Saturday early in September, Mother, Kim and I were having our breakfast on our front balcony. The lake was already full of the weekend fishermen, and the shore beyond our fence was rapidly filling up with them. It did not look like a very peaceful weekend for us. I had noticed in the paper that there was a musical festival in Stresa. I was no fluent newspaper reader, but I had made this out. I suggested that we try our luck, and in no time we were on our way. The drive along the shore of Lago Maggiore was as lovely as ever. By now we had our favourite villas, favourite pieces of statuary, and favourite restaurants built right over the water.

We had always promised ourselves at least one night in one of the big luxury hotels of Stresa. Our luck was in. There was a suite for us. The rooms were so spacious and so charmingly furnished that we almost hated to leave them. Our full length French windows opened onto our own private balcony and gave us a perfect view of Isola Bella. Third-rate hotels in Italy, as everywhere, can be pretty grim, but the luxury hotels give you all the frills, including a phone in your bathroom, a linen cover for your bath mat and even a towel put down at night beside your bed. Home had not been quite like this, and Mother settled in to enjoy the peace and luxury.

The lake called to Kim and me, and soon we were swimming. This was just two hours after leaving home. Each hotel has its own private beach. Somehow there seems to be a special thrill to swimming in Lago Maggiore. The water is so cool and fresh and so clear.

I had a special thrill that morning as some of the guests were certain that I was Italian and complimented me on my English. I was highly complimented to be thought Italian, and as for a compliment for my English, well that was pure delight.

It was one grand weekend, a spur of the moment idea. Our swims were perfection. We explored the city, and Mother had a marvelous time in the shops. We even got tickets for the Zurich symphony. Somehow the music that night sounded as if it was being blown through the string section. It was the first time I had heard string music sound like reed music. We had the added thrill of sitting next to some charming American ladies and having a conversation in English. My Italian was still shaky enough that I delighted in a conversation where I could understand everything. After the concert, we all filed out and down through the now quiet, cool streets to the cafés by the lake. As we settled in at tables and gave our orders for cool drinks and ices, the members of the orchestra, with their smaller instruments in hand, moved in around us. It was so pleasant to be able to thank them for the lovely music they had given.

We lingered over our breakfast on our balcony, enjoying the view of the mountains rising up around the lake, and the different watercraft plying the surface of the water. It was times like this that brought home to us how very lucky we were to be living in Italy as residents, with time to just sit and look and look. When you are a tourist, there is so often a feeling that you must get going and see something else you should not miss, just in case you never come back that way again.

When we found something we loved, we could go back again and again. As we lazed over our breakfast, and saturated ourselves with the view, I could well understand why Stresa was such a favourite spot with Italians and travellers.

When we finally got back home, all was peace and quiet. Giovanni was sitting on a wagon in the barnyard, enjoying the evening and his pipe. As he was an "early to bedder," we stopped to talk. This was one of the nights he had to stay up and watch and wait, for one of his three cows was expecting a calf. Next morning when I went up the lane for our milk, there was a fine calf for me to admire.

There was surprisingly little social life. Our first summer, there were no organized parties and little private entertaining. It did not seem to be the custom in Italy to entertain casually. Wives I met were often very lonely for company, but did not take the initiative and make up a party. We were lucky that scientists who had spent time in Deep River and had a taste of our free and easy type of entertaining did invite us to their homes. I was delighted to meet new people and to see the type of accommodation they had managed to find. We set off one evening to visit a German couple who had acquired a fabulous sounding place up on one of the mountains that looked down on Lago Maggiore. Kim had said, "Now, I want you to make a real impression," so I dressed with special care and chose a bathing suit that was one of his favourites. In Deep River, I had gone swimming at least four times a day and Mother had made me presents of lovely bathing suits. This one was a beauty from Miami.

We met our host and hostess and their children in the boathouse that went with their house. I can only hope that I made a good impression in my clothes, for my bathing suit appearance was a *disastro*. I had washed it the previous autumn, wisely, but far too well. The elasticity was gone and the suit hung limp and pathetic half way down to my knees. It was still a lovely colour, so with as much grace as I could muster, I stepped forth to the dismay of Kim and the quickly concealed amazement of our hosts. I had more than a bit of difficulty staying in the suit, but the swim was wonderful. Were I a poet, I would write odes to the water of Lago Maggiore.

The drive up and up the mountain was spectacular, and their place really a dream. The house was so old that Leonardo da Vinci was known to have visited there. We had the thrill of standing on a spot where he had stood to paint. What we could see of the mountains appears in one of his paintings. There were acres of garden and many fruit trees. We ate fresh apricots right off the trees. There was also *nespole*, a fruit we had found in Italy and loved.

The place was all you could dream of, but they had to pay for the beauty and atmosphere. The drive up the mountain was difficult in bad weather. The water supply could be uncertain, and I knew it was going to be very hard to keep it warm in the winter. However, on that summer evening it was perfect.

As we drove home in the moonlight, Kim was wistfully envious. This was the kind of place he had dreamed of when we dreamed of Italy. I appreciated all the beauty of their spacious villa and their grounds, but I appreciated the smallness of our little pagoda that I knew I could keep clean. With Kim away in Brussels, Mother and I might well be marooned on a mountain top. We had our lovely lake right before us and a bus stop at the end of our lane. I felt our fireplace alone could do much to keep our home warm, and we had oil heat as well. It was hard to have to be practical in the face of all the beauty of Italy, but it was necessary.

When we ordered the firewood for our fireplace, it came piled high in a creaking wooden cart pulled by two oxen. We had some fragrant fires as some of the wood was bayberry. From Giovanni we learned we could buy sacks of hardwood chips from the briar pipe factory. These pieces left over from fabricating the pipes burned like hard coal, slowly and with intense heat. Our fires were one of our delights, and made for cosy entertaining.

All summer we had watched our figs fattening. For us it was exciting. Two fig trees of our very own we had never imagined. When they were plump and succulent, the struggle for the crop commenced. A battle was waged between me and the visiting hornets. I had already learned that anyone passing just reached up and helped themselves as a matter of course. If the hornets had eaten their fill of the honey-sweet fruit, they were little trouble to me. It was when they were hungry and after the fig of their choice that I had to be cautious and courageous. I braved the hornets from an old, tripod ladder that Giovanni had made so long ago that it had become what I call "silverwood."

Everyone had cautioned me never, never to trust a fig tree, as the wood is always treacherous, so I always set up the old ladder.

Not only did I need courage to meet the hornets, but there was a lizard so large, so green and so very quick that he commanded more than respect from me. The lizards we had every day were maybe five to six inches long. This fellow was fourteen inches at least, had a head shaped like a serpent, and he seemed to leap, not dart, about. In spite of this rather fearsome lizard and the hornets, I gathered our fig crop daily as it ripened. We ate them as an *antipasto* with salami or ham and I stewed them as a dessert. The Italians either peel them or open them and suck the insides out. Kim and I found them so good we ate them skins and all. The crop was so plentiful that I bought preserving sealers at Standa, and set about contriving a satisfactory syrup. I was impressed with the wide mouth jars I was able to buy. These preserved figs served as a surprise dessert in the winter, for Italians seem only to eat them fresh or dried.

September and October were golden months. Sad to say, Kim had to report to Canada. He was excited to be going back home, but he was going to miss the winemaking, and Mother and I were going to miss him.

Luckily, a dear friend, Norah, from Edinburgh, had treated herself to a trip to Rome following the Festival, and had then treated us to her company while Kim was away. It was wonderful to see her again and wonderful also to have a companion to go exploring with. There were so many roads I had wanted to walk along, and now it was cool enough for Norah and me to walk daily.

After two weeks of continuous sunshine, the grapes were so ripe we could smell them as we walked the roads. The grapes were harvested in long box-like baskets with handles at each end. These boxes were brought out of barns and lofts and placed in the many little streams that hurry down from the hills to our lake. After they had tightened up in the water (just as the wheels of farm wagons back in Canada would tighten back into the heavy iron rim) the boxes were carried to the vines or taken there by wagon, and then everyone was picking grapes like mad. I saw a group of nuns hard at it, and they were very efficient pickers. We met one dear old couple in Gropello coming home jauntily with a wheelbarrow piled high with purple grapes.

Many of the *contadini* took their grapes to their local *cooperativo*, where a huge, truck affair, not unlike a cement mixer, would arrive. It was called a *macchina di vino*. Norah and I stood in the sunshine and watched baskets and baskets of grapes being dumped into it, and enjoyed the laughter and the joking and the fragrance of the crushed grapes. Later, I was to write Norah that some of this wine cost less than the price of the deposit on the bottles. I was saddened by the huge *macchina di vino*. It took the glamour from a process I had always associated with the Italian way of life. Like so many modern products achieved by modern short cuts, the finished wine did not compare with the home-made wine.

Giovanni had his wine press in the clean small room in the barn where he separated the milk. His was such a potent brew I wondered what effect it might be having on the milk, and how Fritz was standing up to the smell of fermentation. This smell of fermentation was everywhere out in the country when you were near human habitation. We even saw bees tumbling about in what we were certain was a slightly drunken state.

Our house was built in what had been an old orchard and vineyard, and grapes had managed to survive along with our two plum trees, our two fig trees and our sour cherry tree. Kim was going to miss the wine making, but gave himself the pleasure of picking our grape crop before he left. There I was, with a couple of pails brimming over with grapes. Norah grew pale when I started talking about what I should do with them. It seemed she had spent a holiday with friends who had preserved blackberries during the whole time she was with them.

This spurred me on. She should not have this holiday spoiled with my preserving. I went to work with my wide-mouthed Standa jars. As I dashed off jars of jam and spiced grape, I blessed all our friends who had eaten bunches when they had been visiting, for that pocket handkerchief of a kitchen was no place for preserving on a grand scale. I was down to the last batch of jam, wondering what I would put it into, when Angelo, Rina and the boys arrived for a Saturday afternoon swim. That was one batch I did not have to bottle, though in the evening I had to bury a hopelessly burned pot in a far corner of the garden.

During the whole of Norah's visit, we had just one golden day after another. She managed to get quite a sunburn, which speaks well for Italy's fall sunshine. There was a kind of autumn haze, and we seemed somehow suspended in space. There were autumn colours; not vivid ones, more warm yellows and browns. Some of the grape leaves turned a glorious red and the rushes around the lake turned a golden tawny colour.

The fields and fields of corn were allowed to ripen until the cobs burst out of their wrappings. First the corn was picked, and then the roads were paced by gentle, patient-faced oxen pulling home the loads of rustling, dry corn stalks. I assumed they burned some and used some for bedding for the animals.

It was at this time that Norah had the treat of seeing Signor Tamborini and his very fine team of oxen that were his pride and joy. He was always dressed in a sun-faded blue shirt that went so well with his blue, blue eyes. Whenever the load was large and some might fall off, his wife, tall and slim, walked along behind the cart, as is the custom in Italy, and salvaged what fell. They made an unforgettable picture, he so fair and in his old straw hat, and she, so very dark in her black dress. She walked those hard country roads in her bare feet, and I never once saw a wince in her walk. Since they had oxen, she could have afforded shoes. She was unusual in that she walked the roads barefoot and also in that she was tall and slim. Most of the women in our district were short and plump. The men, on the other hand, were usually slim.

While we saw oxen pulling some of the loads of corn husks, we also saw many men and women pulling light wagons themselves. There was always a member of the family following the wagon to pick up anything that might drop off, and to see that no one helped themselves.

I was not certain of all the uses of the corn, but I knew that corn was grown as food for the poultry, and I can tell you that corn-fed fowl is really delicious. Much of the corn is ground into corn meal. The Italians are a great people for tradition and custom. Autumn is the season for *polenta*, a thick cornmeal mush, served at the table piping hot on a wooden board as accompaniment to rabbit or hare. Thick slices are cut off with a wooden knife. The hare or rabbit is cooked in red wine, and the meat goes perfectly with the *polenta*. Rabbit is eaten a great deal in the country. One of my surprises was to see rabbits and chickens sharing the same pens.

Norah and I walked over one day to rent a boat from our friends the Giamberinis. As well as the lumber mill and his picturesque water wheel, he had boats to rent. These boats were a cross between a rowboat and a punt. I had my exercise rowing us over to the island. The story of the duke who had his guests rowed up the lake in a gondola for evenings of pleasure on the island really fired Norah's romantic Scots soul.

As we pushed off for the homeward row, I could point out the summer home of Bruno Martignoni, that long ago had housed the gondola. I rowed us down the lake that Norah might see our place from the water. Suddenly, quite a stiff breeze came up. When you lived near mountains, winds and rains can come up quickly. It was a real pull up to the small wooden pier at Gropello. Sitting waiting for us was an elderly man with binoculars. When the weather had changed, Signor Giamberini had begun to worry that the *signora canadese* might have difficulty. This friend of his had taken the time to sit and scan the water for us. We had been in no difficulty, but it warmed our hearts that someone had been thinking of us and watching out for us.

At the museum in Varese, we visited the room where the lake dweller excavations were on display. They had so much more interest for us, as we had stood where they had been found. One thing that fascinated me about the tools and implements that had been used thousands of years ago was that we had seen *contadini* in the fields around our home using homemade wooden tools unbelievably similar in design.

The romantic story of the island and its parties had appealed to us so strongly that we felt it was most considerate of the museum to have a portrait of the man who had given the parties and maintained a gondola on our lake.

Having shown Norah the island and the archeological finds from there, and the picture of the duke who gave the gondola parties, I had to take her to visit the charming apartment Signor Bruno had made from the boathouse that had housed the gondola. We walked over one sunny afternoon. Norah rather held back from visiting a perfect stranger. But, not only was Norah entranced with the place and how it was decorated, but Signor Bruno was giving a dinner party that evening, and the table was beautifully set. The glasses, the china, everything was in perfect taste. We had a drink with our charming and attractive host and trailed home rather sadly, for it looked as if it was going to be a marvellous party and we wished we could go. To bolster our spirits, I splurged on our dinner. I couldn't bring out any special china or silver, but Norah and I had dressed with such care we had to explain to Mother that it was a form of singing to keep up our spirits, since we could not go to the party down the lake.

While Norah was enjoying our part of Italy, our mail service was causing her considerable distress. Our *porta lettera* she found delightful, but why, when two letters were mailed in Edinburgh at the same time on the same day, did one arrive three days before the other? The British could practically stake their lives on the regularity of their postal system and had developed such a feeling of security in its regularity that any deviation from the norm was almost beyond their acceptance.

Norah was soon to leave and was nervously waiting word from a friend Rhoda, whom she was to visit as she passed through London. We were sitting out in the sun one day when Fritz started barking. His bark was my signal that someone was coming down the lane. It was Maria, and I could tell from the way she was pedaling her bicycle that it was special news. Maria and I had become good friends in Giannina's kitchen while we waited for our milk. Maria had been shopping in the cooperativo in Calcinate when Norah's telegram arrived and she offered to bring it, although it was out of her way, and it was her lunchtime. She waited, all smiles, and was dismayed at Norah's reaction. Poor Norah! Our postal service had upset her, but our telegraph service completely shattered her. The telegram read "SON LONDRE FORTE OTTOBRE LOVE ROODER." When Norah was reunited with Rhoda (I liked the name Rooder), she wrote to tell me that "SON" had somehow come out of "expect you." The moral of this is if your telegram is to be phoned in Italy to someone who speaks no English, try to send it in Italian.

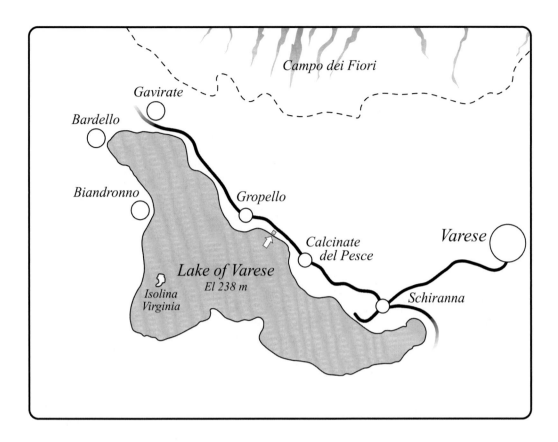

A simplified map of the Lake of Varese, showing the city of Varese and the main towns and villages described in the story. Our Villa was on the shore of the lake between Gropello and Calcinate, and is indicated by the arrow.

Spring, 1961: Kate as she looked at the start of our plans for Italy.

Spring, 1962: The Lake of Varese seen on looking west from the Kursaal Palace Hotel in Varese. Monte Rosa and the chain of the Alps cannot be seen for haze.

Summer, 1962: Our first day at the villa on the Lake. Kate takes a moment from unpacking to savour the view from our balcony. She has just transplanted the azalea from its pot to a place in the soil beside the house. She is looking southwest across the lake to Biandronno, where the church has a lovely chime of bells.

Summer, 1962: A view of the palace of the Duke of Este, now the municipal offices of the City of Varese. We are looking from a hilltop in the extensive gardens of the palace, now a municipal park. The Hotel Europa is out of sight across the road from the palace.

Summer, 1962: An outdoor laundry tub in the countryside on the way to Ispra.

Winter, 1963: Bologna, the Neptune fountain in winter; not the usual postcard view.

Spring, 1963: We had lunch in one of the restaurants spanning the autostrada between Milan and Bologna.

Spring, 1964: Lago Maggiore, seen from the southern extremity of the lake, looking north toward Switzerland. The start of Leonardo da Vinci's canal can be seen.

Spring, 1964: Giovanni's barn seen from Mother's balcony, looking up the hill toward the Villa Bottini, hidden in the trees. The barn is placed to get the most of the winter sun, particularly the upper story, which is used for drying. The ornamental brickwork not only adds to the appearance of the barn, but enhances circulation of air in the upper story. Kate is waving to the camera from our gate. The barn has been converted into a comfortable home, inherited by Gianfranco from his father, Giovanni.

Spring, 1964: This is Kate's friend, the Signora Maria Zanetti, standing in the doorway of her daughter's shop in Calcinate to say goodbye. She has her granddaughter, Giovanna, with her. Giovanna is between eight and nine in this picture. She is dressed for school. Her schoolwork was always exemplary, and she stood at the head of her class.

Spring, 1964: This view of the cathedral at Orvieto came as a surprise. The entire face of the cathedral is decorated in glittering mosaics. The architecture is an interesting combination of gothic and Romanesque.

Spring, 1972: Elevenses at the Socrate Bar in the Piazza Monte Grappa. Kate's favourite STANDA department store forms the backdrop to this picture. STANDA is no more, though the building looks today very much as it did when this picture was taken. The picture is dated by the mens' hats. Their faces are typical of Varese businessmen, however, and can be seen today. The Socrate Bar is gone, and the bus route runs through where these tables used to be. Life is busier, too, than it used to be.

Summer, 1983: In 1983 we went on a two-week cruise in the Adriatic with Angelo and Rina on the 14 meter sloop, "Taboo." This picture was taken in the harbour in Ancona aboard "Taboo," where Kate is talking to Massimo Belisario, the young sailor who brought the sloop down single-handed from Trieste. The conversation lasted no more than an hour, but left Massimo completely under Kate's spell. He remained a faithful friend for years, and always referred to this conversation as milestone in his life.

Summer, 1995: Kate made a last visit to Italy in 1995. Here she is on her beloved Lago Maggiore on the ferry leaving Laveno.

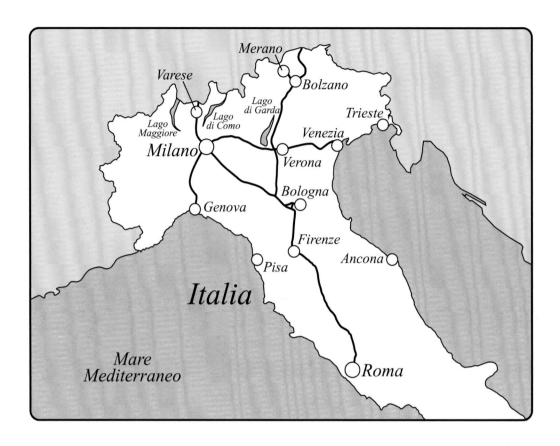

A simplified map showing the main Italian cities and towns visited in this story. Kate took her sister Lib on a tour embracing most of them.

Chapter 7

Autumn Tours

With October, the children started back to school, girls and boys alike attending grade school in black smocks that buttoned up the back. In the spring, the smocks changed to white. All wore coloured bows under an Eton collar, the colour being a matter of personal choice. At the end of the school day, I often saw some of the livelier boys going home with the bows at a very rakish angle around on the shoulder. In our district, they went all day Saturday but had free time on Thursday.

The grade school takes children from five to eleven. Then they are supposed to go on to high school until they are fourteen. Sad to say, most of the children in our district started apprenticeship in our local factories, learning to make pipes, furniture, or leather products. Some of them were bright and would have profited from more education. During our six weeks in Varese, I came to appreciate how very quick and intelligent the boys were who delivered the early morning rolls. They would make good bakers, I know, but I wondered what they might be with more education.

There was a small charge for high school of about $13.00 to cover taxes, upkeep of school sports, report cards and heat. This seems a small charge, but when you remember that in our province of Varese, with a population of 60,000, the average income in 1962 was $854.50. School tax, plus paying for transportation was more than many could afford.

High school hours in Varese were 8:30 a.m. to 1:00 p.m., six days a week. Many Italian mothers never go out in the afternoon, to be sure that their young study. High school teachers are often married women without children, or with children cared for by their grandmothers.

When school started, I really missed Carmella and Enrico. She was nine, very thin and very quick and bright. Everyone said of her,"Oh, she is *furba*." This is a semi-compliment in that it means the cunning and smartness you associate with a fox. Enrico was five, easy-going and plump. Carmella took wonderful care of him as they played by the roadside under the cedars of Lebanon or down by the lake. Their father worked in the rubber conversion plant, and their mother was devoted to them. Every morning, when they were going to school, she rode them into Gropello on her bicycle, and in bad weather she called for them. Since she was a heavy woman, this was work, a real labour of love. Just bicycling herself was work enough, but with two children aboard it really took energy.

The children were just back to school when Kim returned full of news of home and pictures of family and friends. He seemed hardly to be back when he had to go to Bologna on business. He decided to drive, and to take Mother and me with him. I was doing last minute household jobs on a sunny Saturday, and Kim was finishing his packing when our handsome Signor Bruno arrived for a visit. Signor B. was delighted we were to visit Bologna, one of his favourite cities. I got the general idea that the girls and the food in that city were really something extra special. He also told Kim an off-colour story or two about Bolognese women.

Perhaps it was the effort of trying to keep up with this conversation, but when we got to Bologna, Kim discovered that he had forgotten to pack any underwear. This presented a real problem for me, as he had a very full schedule of work, and it fell to me to venture forth and buy men's underwear, not the easiest job when sizes are different and you are not fluent in the language.

The drive to Bologna was exhilarating. After the narrow, often tortuous, roads in our district, driving on the *autostrada* between Milan and Bologna was breathtaking. These wide, straight highways bring out all the Italian love of speed. It seemed to me they felt that they were in a chariot race. We made very good time ourselves.

The land was flat, flat, and all the streams and fields were bordered with poplars. The number of poplar trees was one of my Italian surprises. They are fast growing, and grown for their cellulose. The plastics of Italy are among the finest.

Another feature of the landscape are the many plane and willow trees. These have all their branches pruned off to supply kindling for the kitchen wood-stoves, and are also used in making woven enclosures for protection of the late fall and winter gardens. The trunks of these trees become very thick.

It was October, yet the fields were so green people were gathering crops of clover. I saw three young children helping their father, yet making a game of their work. I saw huge tractors working in the larger fields, yet men in the same fields were doing work with shovels. Women with handkerchiefs tied under their chins and hats atop the kerchiefs, were busy working for the Department of Highways, planting the island between the east and west bound traffic. They wore skirts, not slacks.

As we neared Bologna, the grapes were grown over trees and out along wires running between the trees. In the outskirts of Bologna itself, dear little donkeys with such friendly faces were pulling wine kegs on carts. These wine kegs were long and graceful in shape, with beautiful wrought iron scrollwork on the hoops.

Bologna was a delightful surprise. Many friends had told us of the wonderful food. We knew Bolgnese women used to boast that they spent their whole day rolling pasta and preparing the complicated fillings that go into their *tortellini* and their *agnellotte*. Our bachelor friends had prepared us for the girls and women, who are as beautiful as they are reputed to be, but no one had prepared us for the atmosphere of this most interesting and impressive city. It is exclusively of brick, that old, narrow, Roman brick. The city is coloured in various shades of brown, like the brick from which it is built. There is much traffic, yet the medieval galleries that line the streets give a feeling of peace.

The city has a wealth of Romanesque and Gothic churches, and interesting museums and art galleries. The wife of one of the university staff gave me a tour of the most interesting places. I had time to revisit and savour many of them. The men Kim worked with saw to it that we wined and dined in the tradition that has made Bologna famous. Two of these meals were one too many for Mother, but she recovered in time to go to *Il Pappagallo* (the parrot) a restaurant all tourists must visit. There I saw photographs of the movie stars that had been idols when I was in my teens. They had left in their own handwriting their impressions of this famous restaurant, and of the city. I was having such pleasure in Bologna that it delighted me that they had not missed it in their tour of Europe.

While Kim worked days, I toured the city on foot and Mother came on short jaunts with me. I would walk down for a look at the Neptune fountain, the "Giant" as he is nicknamed. I had the time to stand and feel him dominate the square with his trident, standing over a fountain into which four sirens on dolphins pour water from ewers.

I found the public buildings so handsome that I never tired of looking at them. The shape of the windows and the stone detail around them I found most attractive. I was drawn back many times to the wall of the city hall, where one may see, reproduced along the walls, the faces of almost all the people who gave their lives for their city in the resistance movement during the war. I kept studying their faces, especially the young girls and boys, wondering what they had done and where in these streets they had lost their lives.

I was fascinated with the leaning towers, going many times to where they stand in the centre of the five roads leading out of the city, each road passing through a gate in the old city wall.

Parts of this wall remain, and I was always thrilled to come upon a piece of it between buildings. One of the towers, finished in 1119, is 320 feet high and leans four feet out of the perpendicular to the west. The other (unfinished) is 156 feet high and leans ten feet to the south. My father was a self-taught architect and all of his six living children have a great interest in buildings. I sent a postcard of these leaning towers to my brother. I do not remember receiving an answer to any of my missives to him, but these brought an immediate reply by airmail: "What do you mean, sending me a picture of those towers with no explanation?" I could not give him much of an explanation as I never received very satisfactory answers to my questions, but I wrote and told him that Bologna had at one time 180 of these towers, built by wealthy, powerful families. I couldn't see why they would need so many watchtowers. They seemed very close together to be used in defence, and yet really terrific if they were just status symbols. I found paintings showing early Bologna to be fair bristling with them.

Coming back from looking up at the towers one day, I ducked down into an underpass crossing to avoid the heavy traffic at Via Rizzoli, and there, preserved in the wall, were the Roman mosaics discovered during the construction of the underpass. Sometimes it is a good idea not to read your guidebook too carefully, for then you may meet lovely surprises, as I did that morning.

I was delighted to find that the University of Bologna, which was teaching as early as 1070, had employed many women. Novella d'Andres, of the fourteenth century, was said to be so lovely in form and face that she had to teach from behind a curtain so as not to distract the students. Laura, a mathematician and scientist who lived from 1711 to 1788, managed in the seventy-seven years of her life to become renowned as a professor, and also gave birth to twelve children. I learned that, in 1144, Vacarius went from this university to found the law school at Oxford, and from that time many English and Scots had served as Rectors at Bologna. The Spanish College had been established here at the height of Spanish power in the Mediterranean, and was still attracting students from Spain. Cervantes had been a student here.

As soon as we knew we were to go to Italy, we had started saving our holidays that we might spend them in Italy. Florence is just 125 kilometres south of Bologna, so when Kim's business was finished, we drove down through the Appenines to Florence. It is a beautiful drive. There were autumn colours, not vivid or bright, more soft and hazy in hue. There were grape vines everywhere. Mother was so eager to get to the famous goldsmith shops that have lined the Ponte Vecchio since the sixteenth century that she had no desire to linger over lunch. She was not disappointed in the shops, but the prices everywhere she considered high. Florence has always been a goal for tourists, and with the tourist, up, up go the prices. Here in Florence, we went through art galleries and museums with hundreds of others. In Bologna, there were often only the guards and myself. Kim and I had spent much time in the art galleries when we were in Florence on holiday from Edinburgh. So now, when Mother had rests, we chose to wander through the Boboli gardens. They have been growing ever more beautiful since

1550. We delighted in the pools, the trees, the fountains and the statuary.

As we walked back through the city, we came upon a small leather factory housed in what had been a fine old villa. The elegance of the paintings on the ceiling of the main room and the fine old arch on the street outside let us know that this back street had been at one time a street of great importance. Here we found the friendliness and kindness that meant Italy to us. We were allowed to watch boxes of fine leather being made. Their main business was in export to the United States, but they sold to us at prices much lower than we had found elsewhere. We later took Mother there to see the fine work being done, and to let her enjoy the ceiling and the impressive arch out in the street.

There were a pair of obelisks in the square in front of our hotel, separated by about fifty yards. My guess was that they were used in chariot races. I was thrilled to find that I was right. Florence used them to duplicate races as they were run in Rome. In the Uffici Palace, we found a picture painted on the ceiling of one of the rooms, showing our square and the chariot races in progress. For me, finding paintings showing the life of the cities in earlier times gave me the thrill of being allowed to step back into the past. I could study which buildings were just the same now, which were new and how some had been changed over the centuries.

Mother was dazed by the wealth of art in Florence. Room after room of priceless paintings hung three and four deep on the wall. And on the ceiling yet more paintings. Since we had the car, we could, at leisure, drive her to where she could look down on the city and take in the famous black and white marble Duomo.

There is a very old Etruscan cemetery in Florence, dating from a thousand years before Christ. Here you may also see the coats of arms of the guilds. There was a star-shaped design in the coat of arms for innkeepers, and I wondered if it was too far-fetched to imagine that we had derived our star system of rating hotels and restaurants from this old guild design.

Kim and I would have given the restaurant in our hotel five stars. Normally, we try as many different restaurants as we can, but Mother had taken a tumble and was confined to the hotel, so we found it easier to eat in the hotel dining room. I had a book of Aunt Dorothy's, giving us the regional dishes, cheeses and wines of all Italy. This had proved to be an "open sesame" for us. When, at our first meal, we had asked for some of the specialties of Florence, our waiter must have thought, "Now here are people who really know food." Many of the dishes we were served were not on the menus, but he and the chefs must have decided we should not leave their fair city without tasting all their gourmet specialties. The only time we deserted him was the one time we went to the "Buca Lapi" for one of their famous Florentine steaks.

I could understand Mother at her age preferring the food she was used to, but it saddened us when a young American couple confided to us that they had found the best way to eat was in the bar, where "you could get club sandwiches that were almost like home." As for us, we anticipated each meal to see what treat our waiter would have in store for us. We did not have to order, he just brought us things. At first, we thought he had a speech difficulty, but then we discovered that the people of Florence lisp in pronouncing Italian words. It sounds rather elegant once you are used to it.

He had been giving his wonderful service and advice when we heard a sweet voice say in English: "Just one more question. Is it safe to eat the salad?" Poor man! He gazed at the green salad he had been tossing so lovingly and wondered how anyone could doubt its goodness. He had never heard of the old warning to travellers: "Never trust the greens."

As we drove out of Florence, I wondered where the Villa Lemmi might be. I had heard how, in 1873, the owner had noticed traces of painting under the whitewash of one of the rooms. It had turned out to be a series of frescoes by Botticelli. The villa had belonged to the Torabuoni family from 1459 to 1591, and, while it was in their possession, Botticelli had painted there.

It was a glorious day, bright and sunny, and we passed women carrying big plastic containers of laundry quite amazing distances to lines where the clothes would get the most sun. All the housewives seemed to be making use of that sunshine to air everything they possessed. There were sheets, blankets and open umbrellas. This airing is a passion in Italy and Switzerland. In our neighbourhood I got to know the clothes that were aired so well that I knew when someone had a new nightdress.

Women's dresses and men's suits were usually aired after a wearing, often hung out on an upstairs balcony. Many Swiss hotels even have a little place rigged up outside the window where you may air clothes.

Since the drivers on the *autostrada* drove so very fast and since the sun was so very bright, Kim thought it wise to pull into one of the parking zones. While he closed his eyes to rest them and Mother had a cigarette, I went for a bit of a walk. On the *autostrada* these "lay-bys" are prettily landscaped and well cared for, but the Italians prefer a meal of at least four courses to a picnic, so the picnic facilities are used mostly by foreign travellers. The Germans seem to be great campers, and you often see English families as well.

Few trucks stop at these places, for, while one man drives, the other can sleep in his bed in the cab if he is weary. On this lovely day there was just me and an attendant working on one of the flower beds. I welcomed any chance to practice my Italian and, being an Italian, he welcomed any chance to talk. We were soon chatting away, haltingly on my part and volubly on his. He informed me that he knew a little English, and proudly gave me his few words in a strong American accent. He assured me that he had known more but that it was fading from him. He was, and always had been, a gardener. There was a great gentleness about him. The war had come, and he was forced to become a soldier. He had been taken prisoner and had learned his English in an American prisoner-of-war camp in New York State. He gave me the feeling of such innate goodness and kindness that the thought of his ever having been considered dangerous enough to be shipped across the Atlantic Ocean and kept prisoner seemed ludicrous.

As we sped on home through the flat farmland, Kim and I talked of war. Surely if only we could all travel more and get to know the people of other countries, to wage war would be more difficult. Kim and I agreed that we could never fight against Italy. The thought of Kim on one side and Angelo on the other was impossible. To wound Giovanni or to drop a bomb on the Bottini's villa! No, no! It would be impossible for us.

As we talked, Kim had to keep his eyes on the road and the fast moving traffic, but I was studying the farm layouts. The large plaster and brick barns were always placed so that the open upstairs section had full benefit of the best sunshine. The top half of the barn has the southern wall left open so that the hay and fodder may be kept dry. There is also a good supply of twigs up there drying for starting the kitchen fire. There were great splashes of golden yellow where the corn was hung out to dry. Kim told me that, in China, in the autumn, they say a peasant may have a home like the emperor's, for he has a roof of gold.

When we drew into Varese it seemed almost incredible that we had breakfasted in Florence and that in the later afternoon I could be shopping for our supper in Varese. When we turned down our lane, there was Giovanni by the barn busily weaving rushes into a mat. He explained that, in the fall, the *contadini* gather rushes from the edge of the lake and weave them into mats. These mats were placed as protection over the winter crops to provide fresh salad greens in winter.

Soon after our return, our septic system, after a period of increasingly faltering performance, just gave up all together. It was discovered there was no septic tank at all. Some extremely optimistic soul had laid about three feet of broken weeping tile under our driveway, and that was it.

Out came our fashionably dressed agent, Signor Bruno, who looked at this grave oversight with amazement. There was a very sharp conversation with the builder and then, with his usual gusto and enthusiasm, and the help of two fishermen, he installed a small septic tank that really worked.

It was most unusual when we were in Italy to find a man with any education or wealth who did not consider physical work almost a kind of disgrace. Fashion plate though he was, Signor B. could and did throw himself wholeheartedly into any job. As we got to know him better, we discovered that he had had a somewhat chequered career. I expect he had taken on many jobs that may well have accounted for his versatility and willingness to tackle any work. It was not a trait to be found often. Like so many Canadian and American men, Kim was a handyman and could do repairs and build things, and thought nothing of it. Once when he was repairing an urgently needed electric stove for the Bottinis, I caught a look of shame on our host's face. I wondered if he thought Kim was demeaning himself by the work, but found out later that he had studied the principles involved in the job, and should have been able to do it himself. A workman in one trade did not branch into another type of work as freely as we do in America. A thing our Italian friends found rather strange about our way of doing things was the way we would work together on committees for community affairs. The Italian has his work and his home life, and is inclined to marvel at our ability and willingness to work together in groups.

One day Kim came home and said: "I had lunch today with a Dutch chap named Reinier I liked very much, and I am sure you will too." The Dutch chap apparently went home and said to his

Italian-Austrian wife, Bimbi: "I have just met a chap I can really talk to, and I would like to have him over."

Thus began a new friendship. We had found the enthusiasm and interests of the Dutch very like our own, and Bimbi had an enthusiasm that was infectious. They had an apartment on the outskirts of Gavirate so they were close enough to just drop in. They were too busy to do it often, but it was so pleasant to once more have the odd casual unplanned visit.

One Saturday morning when Bimbi was in Milan visiting her Italian grandmother, Reinier arrived to see what we were doing. We were raking leaves, but in no time we had rented a boat in Gropello and were rowing around the lake. After my efforts to row Norah, I sat back like a queen and let the two men have their exercise. I had made a snow pudding bright and early that morning, and, on the strength of it, invited Reinier to stay for lunch. He was quite transported by that pudding. It was fun to give people new foods and oh, so good, to have friends drop in. In the more formal Italian culture, we had missed the pleasure of having unexpected friends arrive. Even when an Italian had been invited to our house, he would never cross the threshold without saying "*permesso*." In our two years in Italy, Angelo came to our house like family, especially in summer when, like many Italian mothers, Rina took the boys to the mountains for July and to the seaside for August. No matter how often Angelo made the trip up the stone steps to our living room, he never once entered without saying "*permesso*."

Bimbi and Reinier seemed almost like Canadians, and spoke English, so they were a real joy to Mother. Bimbi had grown up in Merano, in the Italian Tyrol. She and Reinier told us so enthusiastically about the mountains, the castles, the wonderful air and the apple trees in blossom in the spring, that we could hardly wait to visit. They told us that many of the noble families of Europe had found it so completely to their taste that they had built castles to come to for part of the year. Since the war, many were living there the whole year round. Bimbi really fired us with her enthusiasm, and we were just waiting for a chance to visit this fabulous place.

With the fall came the hunting season, and the keenness for hunting among Italian men was another surprise for me. They went in for very sporty hunting outfits and hunted our neighbourhood day after day. They, without a glance at us, climbed our fences and their dogs swam around and joined them. They crossed and recrossed our property and all they could hope to scare up were small birds or, with great luck, a rabbit. When I thought of the deer or moose they might get in Canada, this endless pursuit seemed strange. This dead serious hunting continued day after day, and there was never a pleasant *buon giorno* from the hunters, just the marvelous attire, guns at the ready and eager dogs. The hunters took the attitude that since game may have crossed your property or be on it, they have a perfect right to be there also.

Little songbirds may be good to eat. I suppose they are, for certain shop windows had row upon row of their little corpses packed into trays. I could not bear to look at them. Once my eye caught sight of a whole row of beautiful kingfishers, smaller than our Canadian birds, and a brilliant emerald blue. I had never seen more than two of these birds at a time, and the blueness of their feathers took my breath away.

With the cooler weather, we frequently made Saturday trips to Lugano, because cigarettes were taxed so highly in Italy that Mother's brand (Chesterfields) were prohibitively expensive. The trip from Varese took only an hour, and going over to buy gas and cigarettes was a weekend outing for many. We were always sure of meeting people we knew. On one trip, while I made a necessary stop at the post office in Varese, Mother had a cigarette in the car and Kim slipped into a favourite little nearby bar for his "Punt e Mes," one of the myriad Italian drinks. At this bar, you sat outdoors in an ancient courtyard that had been part of a convent in 900. So many carts had passed through over the years that there were groove marks in the old stones.

When I came to join Kim, I spied a jar of preserved grapes and managed to get across to the proprietor that I had eaten *uva-pas*, a grape delicacy, in Sorrento, and had found them simply delicious. He was all smiles, and saying,"Wait, wait," he dashed into a back room and returned with bunches of drying grapes for me. I asked if I could pay for this treat. "No, *un regalo, un regalo*" (a gift, a gift). He had been so very generous that I could not possibly eat them all, even with help from Kim, and I wondered if one was permitted to take grapes across the border.

We usually crossed at Ponte Tresa, and as we crossed over the bridge, I always had to look back over my left shoulder for an enterprising fisherman who had a very long pole and used to fish from a second storey window. I always hoped that I would see him catch a fish through that window but I never did. When we got to the customs, I found I could keep my grapes. The only thing you could not take across the border was fresh meat.

Walking along the park beside the Lake of Lugano, we approached a monument that I expected to be of some European figure of history that I would not know. Imagine our surprise to find it was indeed a man we knew, for written in Italian script (this part of Switzerland speaks Italian) was "Giorgio Washington." We had no idea why Lugano would erect such a fine monument to George Washington. Since Lugano did so well out of the tourist business, Kim suggested that perhaps Giorgio had invented the American tourist, and hence the tribute to him.

We usually took the Valganna route to and from Lugano. Valganna means valley of the Ganna river, and it is a most picturesque drive through a gorge and then into open countryside, with always the mountains to look up to. At one particularly sharp bend, there was a little white cross and a bouquet of flowers. Sometimes we would see a couple of young men putting fresh flowers by the cross. I wondered if someone had been killed at this spot during the war, or if it had been a traffic accident. Family love, or just love, is so strong in Italy, that in our two years of using that road I can never remember seeing that white cross without flowers beside it.

With the cooler autumn mornings, we were waking to the wonderful smell of wood-smoke. We had no close neighbours, but the smell of fires being kindled in wood stoves came in our open balcony doors every morning. Giannina's kitchen had become so much a part of my life that I could lie in bed and see her, in my mind's eye, opening the iron door of her stove, putting more kindling in and moving some of the big pots she was always using to brew some kind of mash for her turkeys.

With the autumn also came fog. I had heard that Milan and the area around could have five months of fog, but I had not realized Varese would have them too, or that it could be so dense. We did not have it for five months, but when it did come, it was so thick that first Giovanni's barn would disappear, and then even the lake would be gone. We were wrapped in a world of quiet, quiet gray. I was always thrilled to hear the dip of fishermen's oars in this muted world. The church bells came through clearly, and we could hear bells we had never heard before.

When we had fog, I could not help but worry about Kim driving. During a bad fog in 1961, six men at Ispra had lost their lives in driving accidents. When it became late, I could not keep myself from taking up a watching post at our kitchen door. Now that the trees were leafless, I could see the lights of cars coming from Gropello. When I finally saw welcome lights coming down our lane, I would turn to my stove with a great sigh of relief. We had had fog in Edinburgh, but in our part of Italy fog came more often and lasted longer.

It was in the autumn that the shepherds brought their sheep from the northern mountains down through Italy, some going as far south as Abruzzi, which is not far from Rome. Kim and I knew nothing of this custom and were wakened one night from a vivid dream of sheep, to hear every dog in our neighbourhood barking wildly and the night air full of the bleating of sheep. We could not believe our ears. Next morning, we could hardly believe our eyes. We saw hundreds of sheep. They were all up the tiered hillside next to Bottini's, and were eating everything they could reach, even when they had to balance precariously on hind legs to reach the morsel they wanted. There were two shepherds and, as always, at least one donkey. Newborn lambs were put in pouches slung to the donkey's saddle when they were too young to make the next march. The bleating mothers never left the donkey's side when their young were in those pouches. As I have noted, Italians can be cruel to animals. I have seen a shepherd beat his dog when it was all I could do to keep from trying to beat the shepherd. The shepherds live a nomadic life with the sheep, pasture them by the roadside or in unfenced fields, and the donkeys carry their few possessions along with the newborn lambs. Many Italian motorists love to meet a flock of sheep on the road. The prayer is "press close to my car, O sheep." The lower parts of the car get a cleaning they could get in no other way. The parts rubbed by the sheep are left shining with lanolin and the sheep do not seem to get any dirtier.

Once during the sheep migration I was waiting for the bus by the little bridge under the persimmon tree, and I saw two shepherds skin a sheep. It was the quickest, neatest thing I had ever seen. I did not know if the sheep had died lambing or if they had killed it, but as I waited for my bus there were a few quick cuts, and the sheep was pulled out of its woolly skin almost as neatly as a woman pulls off her gloves. The skin was hung on a leafless peach tree and one of the shepherds strode off towards Gropello, the carcass flung over his shoulder. I wondered if it was to be payment for all the grass the sheep had eaten, or if he was heading for the tiny butcher shop.

While the skinning was going on, the sheep kept a respectful distance and, I felt, looked none too sure of themselves. I climbed onto my bus a bit shaken myself. When I left the house to shop in Varese, I had never expected to see a sheep skinned right at the bus stop. Life was always surprising me in Italy.

Chapter 8

Our First Winter at the Lake

One of my most delightful surprises was finding Bruna. I learned, in Giannina's kitchen, that she had a friend in Calcinate who could speak English. This friend was Bruna, and we sat next to each other one day on the bus. The English Bruna spoke was mainly "I remember leetle, I forget much," and "You understand?" She had a beautiful pronunciation of "lovely."

She had gone to England after the war to work in a glove factory. She had not remained long and had little contact with the English, but she treasured the words she had learned. When she returned to Italy, she had married a widower with three children, and had borne him a daughter, Maria Louisa, who was seven when I met her. Bruna's husband was ill with muscular dystrophy, so more and more work was falling on her uncomplaining shoulders. She was a dynamic person, so vitally alive you could almost feel an electric current from her. She kept house for the six of them. The two young men had followed their father's trade as plasterers, a good trade to have in Italy.

145

The daughter, Celestina, was part of the bicycle parade that made its way from Calcinate to the furniture factory in Gropello. Bruna had them all home for *la colazione* at midday, and did all the work for them. She also kept three cows. I would meet her on the road pulling home a wooden cart piled high with hay that had been stored in the stone hut on their piece of land. Her cow shed was sweet and clean. How she loved those cows! When one kicked her, she made sure that I understood that it had not been the cow's fault. She showed me how it was that her wedding ring had pinched the cow while she was milking and had aggravated the cow into kicking her.

I never knew how she managed it, since she had so much work to do, but quite often she and I sat side by side on the bus. One of her reasons for going into Varese was to put money into a bank account for her beloved Maria Louisa. Bruna was always happy and just radiated good humour and energy. Immediately we became good friends, and I was welcomed to her home, which was beside the church in Calcinate in a series of homes that honeycombed the little hillside. You entered a small, open portico that contained the laundry tub. No stream ran through this village, and there was no public wash place. Each family had the laundry tub at the door. Part of the year this portico was shared with skimming swallows who built their mud nests against the walls. The kitchen door opened onto this enclosure, and it was in the kitchen where the family lived. They used an outside stone staircase to the second floor rooms where they slept and dressed.

From the portico, another door led down to Bruna's three fine cows. Just beyond their shed, and built into the back of the house, was the family toilet, a very simple affair with running water. The family washed at the open laundry or in the kitchen. Sometimes when I came to visit, Bruna would be hard at work in the kitchen, rolling out and cutting fresh pasta for noodles, or her sewing machine would be whirring away.

I made quite a few friends on my bus trips, but none like Bruna. I always enjoyed these trips. The bus drivers and the ticket-taker always had time for fun. Once we were getting settled in with our shopping, and one of them said, "Anyone got anything for me to eat?" Someone offered him *grissini* (dry bread sticks) and he said, "I am not that hungry, thank you."

I remember a lady climbing on once and asking if it was the bus for Osmate. He said,"Yes, Signora, but today we are going by way of Milan." She, as well as the whole bus, had a good laugh at the thought of a sixty kilometre detour.

I would try to follow discussions that might involve as many as half the people on the bus. It was on my shopping trips that I realized what a passion the Italians have for rhetoric. It so appeals to them, that it does not seem to make a demand on the mind.

The English want to understand, but often the Italians seem to care more about emotion, the effect the sound has upon them. There were times when they sat back and let the talk flow about them, and other times when they were saying repeatedly *"ho capito, capito"* (I understand, understand). I would be so busy trying not to miss anything that I would forget to say *"ho capito,"* and then Bruna would say in English, "You understand?"

I noticed the Italians did not interrupt each other as much as we do. The person speaking was allowed to have his say. Was I wrong in thinking he was allowed to practise his rhetoric? If it went on too long, the other person would reach out and hold the speaker's hands, and then have his or her say. I know of at least one family where everyone is delighted to talk at the same time. A Roman once told me that even one Italian all by himself is more than capable of creating confusion. I enjoyed the noise, confusion and chatter of my shopping trips, and I blessed my country life. Had we lived in parts of Varese or Milan I might never have had the chance to be part of this aspect of Italian life, for people who wish to protect their privacy can be very aloof and dignified. The country folk wanted company and conversation, and they included me.

Either on the bus, or while shopping, I always seemed to have some adventure or meet someone interesting. Usually at dinner Kim would say "Well, what nice person did you meet today?" or "What adventure did you have?" Once I was convulsed in our bank by a Japanese trying to sell very gaudy, embroidered ties to the very dignified and polite staff. They did not wish to buy, but were so courteous, the poor salesman felt that all he had to do was say *"multo bella"* a little more firmly and faster and surely they would weaken. He was flashing his embroideries about with the speed and skill of a matador, though encumbered with the load of ties over his shoulder.

Another time, I went to a certain *salumeria* to buy a little pork. It was beside a fine old church. This day turned out to be a day of celebration for the saint the church was dedicated to. The church was decorated with gorgeous crimson velvet, and the square was gay with little stalls selling things to eat and the trinkets and baubles that entice at a fair. It was the *"festa,"* the birthday of the Saint, and there was merrymaking and gaiety.

Sometimes I would encounter a funeral procession. These could be very impressive. My heart would be downcast when I would see the tiny, white casket of a young child. Sometimes my encounter might be with a chestnut vendor who was roasting his chestnuts in the top of an oil drum.

My last port of call was the fruit and vegetable shop across from the bus square. What I could carry across the street was more than I could carry down our lane; so I would leave half my load in Giannina's kitchen, if she was in. This way I had two visits with her.

With November came the rain, and how it rained! It rained from the first until the 18th, and it rained night and day. The lake rose and rose and soon was half way across our lawn. Giovanni and our *porta lettera* were always measuring to see how much it had risen.

The constant rain presented me with a real problem. There was no garbage collection in the country, so it behooves each family to get rid of its own. This explains why the streams are garbage filled. In the country villages, where many people live close together and do not have a patch of land to burn or bury refuse, the streams are the only solution, for they are not privately owned. While I could understand the convenience of this garbage disposal, I love standing on a bridge and looking down, so I could never pollute a stream. A garbage pit and a fire were our solution. It was so dark when Kim got home at night that I undertook the garbage fires. Whenever we left on holiday,we had to trek up to the garbage pit to see that all had burned away.

As the rain continued, I was continually crouching over our pit, trying to get my fire started under an umbrella. I had a particularly trying time one morning and then received a letter from a Deep River friend, envying me the thrill of living in sunny Italy. I was more than damp, and my eyes were smarting from the smoke under the umbrella, and I thought: "Ha, ha, if you but knew!"

On November 18, the crowd of Canadians (there were five of them working at Ispra) all went dancing at Bel Sit. As we came out to our cars, the first snow was falling. "Well, how do you like that? I leave Canada to get away from this, and here it is in Italy." Every time I saw the man who made this remark on the ski slopes, I wondered how he could hope to indulge in his favourite sport without snow. I soon learned that you could have spring at the foot of the mountains and skiing at the top. That first snowfall ushered in the coldest winter since 1927. The winter presented real problems to many. We had our share.

Speaking of Bel Sit, a lovely memory comes to mind. Kim and I went dancing there quite often, as dancing is one of our pleasures. A very good orchestra came up from Milan three times a week. One evening the music seemed particularly good to us and we were having a marvelous dance. When we came back to our table, our waiter was holding a choice bottle of wine and said "Will you accept this?" "Certainly" was Kim's response, "but who gives it to us?" " The gentleman over there." We went over to his table and Kim asked "Why are you so kind to us?" "Italians love to see people having a good time" was his reply. When we parted, he bowed and kissed my hand. As always, I had to fight the inclination to curtsey. Although we danced there many more times we never saw him again.

I had a lovely surprise a month later on December 19th. I was scurrying about to get as typical a Canadian meal as I could for Bimbi and Reinier. The smallness of my kitchen presented real problems, and I was doing my usual contriving and conniving. Suddenly, about 4:30, the doorbell rang. I was amazed, as we had so few unexpected callers. I opened the door and there stood the tall, handsome young priest from Calcinate and a young altar boy. They were both in spotless white surplices, trimmed with beautiful lace. There was gold embroidery on their cassocks. My breath was quite taken away by the beauty of their apparel and the church vessels they were carrying. They had walked the mile from the church, blessing all the houses along the way, and their cheeks were rosy from the crisp, cold air. Their eyes were shining. They had just blessed Giovanni's barn and now they had come to bless our home. I could tell the furnishings of our living room, our Canadian pictures, the coziness, the grate fire burning quietly, were as much of a surprise to them as their visit was to me. After they had left I went back to my tiny kitchen undaunted by its lack of working space, for my heart was singing. I just wished that I could have been in the barn when it had been blessed and seen the three cows as they turned their benign faces towards the door to see who had entered the stable.

Early in December, on one of my shopping trips in Varese, I was surprised to come upon two shepherds. They were dressed in coarse herdsmen's clothing, with sheepskin vests and fur chaps like cowboys wear. These chaps came down below their knees and thong laces criss-crossed down from their knees to their soft leather shoes. They wore unusual, gnomish felt hats with coloured ribbons streaming from the peak. One was playing a bagpipe-like instrument made from what seemed to be the tanned lining of a sheep's stomach. I found out it is called a *zampogna*. The other played a whining pipe-like flute called a *cornamusa*. They made me think of startled wild animals. They looked in the store windows as though they were completely unaccustomed to such sights. There was a shyness and a strangeness about them, and people kept a distance from them as they played.

I found out that shepherds come down from the hills in pairs and play this strange mountain music as a homage to the Virgin. This rite takes place during December and ends on Christmas Eve. Shepherds who winter their sheep in Abruzzi go to Christmas Eve midnight service in Santa Maria Nel Arcoeli, on the outskirts of Rome. It is in this church between Christmas and Epiphany that children from Rome are allowed to speak about the Christ child.

Christmas decorations appeared in the stores in December, which pleased me greatly. I hate to be rushed into Christmas right after Hallowe'en. I was impressed with the beauty and elegance of the design and colour in the decorations. Plastic was used most effectively. I never saw a Santa Claus, but in some of the stores a dazzling fairy delighted the children. Just as Italy has so many different dialects, customs and foods, Christmas is celebrated differently in different parts. Villages a few miles apart may have completely different ways of celebrating. In one, the Christmas Fairy takes the place of our Santa, in another the

Infant Jesus. There is a Papa Natale in some and Luciana brings the gifts in others. Christmas trees are not traditional for the season, but many are sold; usually potted small ones complete with roots. There is not a general exchange of gifts, gifts being more for the children. The religious significance of Christmas is strongly stressed.

In our part of Italy, it is at Epiphany that most children receive their gifts, and it is "Befana" who brings them. Befana is a corruption of Epifania. She is an old crone, a kind of witch. She has a hooked nose, a patched apron, a broom and a bag on her back. Legend has it that she once lived in an old caravan route, when three wise men came by following a bright star, and asked for directions to Bethlehem. They said they were taking gifts to a newborn babe. Later a shepherd stopped and told her the babe was the son of God and urged her to go. She was busy with household tasks and by the time she had loaded her shoulder pack and donkey with gifts, the shepherd was out of sight. She was unable to follow his trail, and ever since she goes into all houses at Epiphany, giving to all children, hoping that some day she will find the right one. To bad children she gives ashes, switches, or a lump of coal.

It is the custom in many cities to give gifts to the police at Epiphany and it is a sight to see the policeman, standing on his traffic island, the island piled high with gifts, cakes, wine and toys.

The Italians have a saying. "Spend Easter anywhere you like, but spend Christmas with your family." We had spent four Christmases away from Canada when we were in Edinburgh, but, for some reason, suddenly a desperate loneliness came over us. We missed Christmas carols. There are none in Italy. When you live abroad, you do not feel like a tourist, but the trouble is that you cannot feel yourself a true native. You have a greater sense of wonder in all that you see, but at times you have a great feeling of desolation. We found Italy beautiful, and our lives most interesting, but suddenly, before Christmas, it hit us like a blow that it was not home. As Kim said, one word seemed to describe living abroad at that time: "exile." Feeling as we did, it would have been the logical time for us to go on a sightseeing trip, but to add to our feeling of sadness, Mother was laid low with a very bad flu.

The family had sent a tape recording of a pre-Christmas party. Everyone spoke to us and we heard snippets of conversation that were recorded unawares. Duncan, a great nephew, aged four, suddenly asked why Uncle Kim and Aunt Kate never spoke back. Feeling as pathetically homesick as we were, this was all very hard to take. When Mary, in the most intimate way imaginable, told us of her arrangement of the little angels she had bought in Stresa, I bolted from the room, tears streaming. We really were a sad threesome. There was little we could do, as Mother's flu had to wear itself out, but Kim and I threw ourselves into an Italian way of Christmas.

On Christmas Eve, we went to midnight mass in Calcinate with Giannina, Signora Zanetti and her two daughters. The Zanetti son stayed to serve wine and cigarettes in the shop. During the service at the church, only the choir members did the singing. For me it was very moving to hear sweet old voices, that had once been in the choir, join in from the congregation. The fine voice of the young priest added to the beauty of the service.

I tried hard to be soulful, and to forget that the church was unheated, and that my feet seemed to be gradually turning to ice.

However, when the service was ended, and we all streamed out into the crisp, cold starlit night, they managed to carry me along with the throng that filled the road. The church bell pealed joyously and bells from the churches all around joined in. Everywhere we heard *"Buon Natale, Buon Natale."* We six went back to Signora Zanetti's kitchen in behind the shop, and how I luxuriated in the warmth! We had *pan dolce* and *spumante*, which are as much a part of Italian Christmas as plum pudding is of ours. *Pan dolce* is a special, bread-like cake with raisins and currants. It is eaten by some until Lent begins.

Giannina was a cousin of the Zanetti family, and there was much warm and intimate talk. As Kim and I ate and drank with them and were so much a part of the group, I thought how very lucky we were to have such kind friends.

I thought the same the next day when we spent Christmas afternoon with the Bottini family. Everyone was there. After hours of conversation and listening to records, we left, laden with all kinds of food made specially for the day. The turkey was not roasted and stuffed but appeared in aspic, as an antipasto. All the time I was in Italy, the only stuffing I ever tasted was in an Italian home and was made by a woman who had lived in England for a time. Yet when I served stuffed pork tenderloin as a type of Canadian meat dish, they loved it. Our Christmas meat was Mother's favourite, which she called "Irish turkey," and is a roast of pork.

Our little tree was gay with baubles and red candles, and it completely captivated little Carmella and Enrico. Throughout the holidays they would appear with friends from their school, just to enjoy the tree. Many food stores were open for a few hours Christmas morning, as the Italians are accustomed to shop for food every day. It seemed strange to see stores open on Sunday mornings, but in the small towns bakers baked every day. The bread in Italy has no preservative in it that keeps it soft for days. While some stores were open on Christmas day, it is very hard to find a restaurant, as everyone goes home to be with the family. Another different custom was that it is quite all right to have your Christmas card arrive until the end of January. Many people went dancing New Year's Eve, and as the Italian mothers we knew would leave their children only with family, I realized many grandparents were seeing in the New Year with their grandchildren. I had such pleasure from the church bells at Christmas that I could hardly wait to hear them welcome in the New Year. New Year's Eve has no significance for the church, and no bells are rung. Instead, I heard fireworks popping and guns being fired.

In Southern Italy, it is the custom in the New Year to throw out of the windows old things, plates, glasses, etc., things no longer wanted. In some places it is rather dangerous at New Year's to walk beneath windows.

Some southerners worked at the rubber conversion factory near us, and when I walked along to shop at the *cooperativo* the first week in January, I realized these southern men had thrown out their old rubber boots along the roadside.

After New Year's, the weather became really cold, and one quiet, still, night the lake froze. The ice was as smooth as glass. Our *porta lettera* checked daily the thickness of ice, and I gnashed my teeth in frustration to think of my skates hanging in the garage in Deep River. However, one of our Canadian friends had insisted on lending me skates. They were not going to be used and, luckily, were a perfect fit. So there I was, skating daily in brilliant sunshine on the smoothest ice I had ever known. The only company I ever had was Duke, the Irish setter who lived with Big Maria. Duke could go wherever he wished, but I had promised Kim that I would never go far from the shore and that I would always carry our broom; so that, if the ice broke, I could have a means of getting out. I made this promise to Kim because of the woman in my favourite *salumeria*. She cautioned us so desperately against skating on the lake that her fear made a deep impression on us. It seems that every time the Lake of Varese freezes, it claims a life. We listened to her. I carried my broom and had skating such as I had never dreamed of. Friends along the shore have written to me that, whenever the lake freezes, they miss the *signora canadese* with her *scopa*.

The prophecy of my deeply worried friend in the *salumeria* came to pass that winter. A woman in her early thirties was out walking with her young son and his beloved dog. The pup dashed out onto the ice and went through. What happened from then on I am not sure, but the mother lost her life saving the dog and the boy. We were amazed that our local tragedy was reported in the *Globe and Mail* in Toronto.

With the New Year, Kim and I threw ourselves into skiing with all the ardour of the Italians. We had always enjoyed skiing, but the enthusiasm of the Italians for this sport was one of my Italian surprises. On weekends they came by the hundreds; it seemed by the thousands. There were fleets of rented buses and an unending stream of cars. Many piled their gear on the little motor scooter Vespas and made for a snowy slope. It was quite a sight to see two men, two pairs of skis and two pairs of poles all balanced on a tiny Vespa.

We had been surprised that the Centre at Ispra had organized so few activities to bring the people together, but we were delighted by the organized outings of the skiing enthusiasts. The first weekend we settled Mother into the Albergo Europa in Varese, left our car, and walked across the street to a bus stop and waited for the charter bus. When it came, we piled into a bus full of people: Dutch, French, German, one Spaniard and a Belgian couple. It seemed like a meeting of the League of Nations, with everyone having his say. When the singing started, whatever language it was in, as many as could joined in. I was carried back to boarding school days when we rode in rented buses to games with other schools, or to the theatre. Of course then the only man aboard was the driver, but there was the same spirit of fun and close companionship.

After driving for two hours, we all piled out for a refreshment break. The air was already much colder, and oh, the joy of having a good stretch and a walk, for we were really packed into that bus. By midnight we were all bedded down in a place called Ponte di Legno, Bridge of Wood. The snow was white and deep, the air was crystal clear, the evergreens seemed very tall, and lights down in valleys and up on mountainsides twinkled like stars. There was such a deep quiet that the very stillness seemed to vibrate, to have a pulse. I knew we were high up in a wooden hotel and that the staircase was wood, and if a fire came, what to do? I took a last look at the twinkling lights and felt that we would be taken care of and fell asleep.

We were thrilled in the morning to look out on the little mountain community nestled into the mountainside, and to see the covered bridge. To save us all money, the policy was to get accommodation at inexpensive hotels about an hour's drive from good ski slopes. For a very low price, we had our return bus fare, two night's lodgings, two breakfasts and our Saturday night dinner. Naturally, at this price we did not have private bathrooms; and naturally also there was great traffic in and out of the two toilets per floor. When my turn came, the lock on the door refused to turn to let me out. The bus that was to take us to Passo di Tonnale was waiting below, engine running. I beat on the door and frantically called for Kim who was waiting in our room. He came running and we had a desperate conference through the door. We were short of time, and something had to be done, and done fast. The second toilet, right next door, was empty; and all I had to do was climb out one window and into the next. When I looked down at the sheer drop, I felt I could not do it. But when I thought of the long ride we had taken to get up into this ski country, courage came to me, and I eased myself out of one window. Hanging on for dear life, I came in over the back of the toilet in the next bathroom to be grabbed by Kim who is, if possible, more afraid of heights than I am. We raced down the three flights of stairs and made the bus, but with no time to ex-plain why one toilet would appear to be occupied all day.

As we drove to the slopes, I wondered why it had to be me that got locked in. I am not the most courageous of skiers and my rather shattering climbing experience made me even more cautious that day. I decided not to even try the ski tows, but contented myself with small slopes that I could climb. This first skiing in the higher altitudes left me a bit breathless, but the mountainside was streaked with lines of skiers who seemed to be fired with energy. The sunshine, the snow and the mountain formation would have been worth the trip alone. In my rests and pauses for enjoyment of the scenery, I found myself wondering how Hannibal got his thirty-two elephants up into the Alps.

When you ski high up in the mountains, the length of your skiing day depends on the sun, for until it appears over the mountain it is intensely cold. That day, as soon as the sun went down behind the ridge, the sudden cold drove us all back to our bus. On the drive back, the camaraderie was a joy to experience.

People who loved the outdoors had enjoyed a day of glorious sunshine and exercise. You could just feel the relaxed contentment. The walls of our hotel were so thin that you could even hear the sighs of contentment as people eased themselves into bed for naps before dinner.

Both the bathroom doors were open, I was relieved to see. After dinner (which was very good), I could not get over the reasonableness of our jaunt. Many of us found a spot in the village where we could dance. Kim and I had the first dance together and then a number of teenaged boys there asked me to dance. For the rest of the evening, if I was not dancing with Kim, I was dancing with one of them. I am sure there are very few Canadian teenagers who would ask a mature, older woman to dance, but that evening it happened to me. In Italy, that night at least, if you could dance and were willing, difference in age was no barrier to having fun.

I had not the slightest feeling of being old enough to be a mother, or even a grandmother. We enjoyed dancing and they were as charming to us oldsters as they were to girls of their own age. I realize this was partly because the bonds of family life are so strong in Italy, and partly because they are accustomed to enjoying themselves with older people. It also seems that Italian males, whatever the age, enjoy the society of women.

This weekend was such a success that ninety signed up for the next trip. Two buses had to be rented, and the charge was even lower. This time we drove up into the Dolomites, stayed at a small and inexpensive village, and were on the slopes at Madonna di Campiglio when the sun came over the mountains. One couple came along just to see and enjoy the scenery. They were Chinese, born in Formosa, who had come to Ispra after ten years in the United States. Their faces, amazed and delighted, were a treat to see when Kim spoke to them in Mandarin Chinese. It was wonderful luck meeting them, for the Chinese have a marvelous sense of humour, and for the rest of our stay in Italy we shared jokes. This is more difficult to do in a foreign language and we had all missed this form of fun. Also, they were another couple Mother could talk English with, and we all enjoyed their daughter, Alberta, and their son, Norbert, both very young and very cute.

On this ski trip I made no shattering roof-top trek and managed to pass a milestone by conquering an unreasoning fear of a certain type of ski tow. This meant that I was spared hours of climbing and gained a new confidence which paid dividends in other ways as well. Whenever I found myself in any kind of traffic jam in Varese, I would remember the conquered ski tow and sit out the traffic snarl.

It was also on this trip that I watched a dog carefully bury his bone in the snow. There was nothing but snow around, so he had adapted his need to the conditions. For me it was a strange sight. We were having lunch as we watched him, and it was at that lunch that we made the acquaintance of Grappa, an Italian liquor, which immediately became a great favourite of Kim's. We did not want to miss out on anything so we tried it then and there. I do not recommend it while skiing, as it gives you a confidence beyond your skiing ability.

On the homeward trip, I was most impressed with one of the Italian girls and the sensible and practical way she helped us. Our refreshment stop was also a much needed chance to use the bathroom. The men from our bus were all in and out of their toilet and eating, but due to our ski clothes we were taking so much longer, some of us were not going to have time for anything to eat. This girl stepped over to the men's room, said it was an emergency measure, and that we were taking over. Male newcomers patiently waited while we used their facilities as well as ours.

As soon as we had come to Italy, I had noticed the realistic attitude of many of the Italians. They could take such a practical, sensible view of things and an acceptance of situations. But they combined their realism with great sentiment.

If we wanted just a day's skiing, we could drive to Stresa, which took only an hour, and board a little ratchet train. This train car took us winding through the city and let us look into the gardens of the lovely villas. We could even see the names painted on the dog houses. Then we were out in the open country, chugging up the mountainside to the snowy peak of Mottarone. The trip up took an hour, and if you had not started out with friends, you had often made new ones by the time you reached the ski slopes.

We only went there on a Saturday because the crowd on Sunday was too large for us. Even up there you had a limited time for skiing, and where you might have grabbed a pizza, most of the Italians took time out to have a real Italian dinner. There was antipasto of assorted meats and pickled mushrooms, or hearts of artichoke. The pasta either of noodles or spaghetti was served with a good sauce and liberally sprinkled with cheese. The meat course was usually breaded veal cutlet. The green salad was crisp and good, and there was always bread and cheese and, of course, the wicker basket of fresh fruit and nuts with the bow of ribbon tied to the handle. Real napkins were used, never paper ones. It always amazed us, where everything had to be brought up the mountainside, that they could give such service, leaving out nothing. I was amazed also that during the noon hours, when the sun was at its best and when the non-Italians would have made use of the tows, all the tows stopped running to allow the attendants to eat their important noonday meal at the time they were accustomed to eat. No sandwich lunches were bolted and no shift duties were organized. While I often longed to be on the slopes in the warm noon sunshine, I was delighted that the Italians held to the tradition of their noon meal.

At Mottarone, there was a stone patio on the sunny side of a small hotel where we would sit for the time it took our Italian colazione to digest. It was far larger than we usually ate at noon. One day out on this patio something happened that delighted us. A crowd of Dutch skiers were enjoying the sunshine and their picnic lunches. Afterwards one of the men was helping his wife put her ski boots back on. When they left, a vivacious Italian girl turned to the Italian beside her and said, "Now, why don't you treat me like that and help me on with my boots?" Quick as a wink came back, "All right, go ahead and marry a Dutchman, and when you really want him, where will he be? Standing with his finger in a hole in the dike!" They went on in Italian so fast that I was unable to understand, but Kim said their repartee would have earned them first class wages on radio or TV.

One Saturday, we had a particularly wonderful day of skiing and returned to Mother and our fireside to be brought down to earth with a thud. *Un disastro* had befallen us. Our water had frozen. Kim got out the axe and chopped a hole in the ice that we might have water to wash with, and to flush the toilet. For our drinking water we trekked up to Bottini's. Days of this went on with our agent, Signor Bruno, trying to achieve some sort of running water for us. Kim had to go off to Brussels. Mother and I decided to stay on rather than go to a hotel. We knew we could have coziness and warmth in our own place. The unusually cold weather was making heating a real problem, but our furnace and our grate fire never let us down. Each morning I had to chop open my water hole as it froze over every night. One day as I came in over the ice with my pails of water with bits of green algae floating about, Signor Bruno once more turned up to tell me he was working to achieve running water for us. He gallantly complimented me on my pioneer spirit. By the time Kim got back, my spirit was flagging. Giovanni had been wonderful about bringing down drinking water, and would have tried to keep us in lake water, but he had a full day of his own and, with the extreme cold, all outside workers had more to do. I had come to the time when the most perfect thing I could think of would be to turn a tap and see water flow out. Mother and I were just dreaming of baths. We decided we would have to give in and go to a hotel. We still had holidays, so we decided to spend our hotel money in a ski resort. Mother in a ski resort seemed a bit strange, but we knew she would be warm in the rather posh hotel we had in mind.

Friends had given me beautiful plants at Christmas, azaleas and fuschia. I could not leave them behind and did not want to bother friends with the care of them. I packed them warmly in cardboard boxes and up into the Dolomites and to Madonna di Campiglio they went with us. I wondered what the staff might think of me. The porter who carried them up to our room exclaimed, *"Che bella, che bella,"* and made me feel it was the most natural thing in the world to bring lovely plants along to enjoy at a ski resort.

The first thing I did was to fly to the bathroom for the sheer joy of seeing water that I had not carried. Mother and I gloried in the baths and the chance to get caught up with a bit of washing. One hotel had its plumbing freeze, and we waited apprehensively, but ours never let us down. The skiing was wonderful, the food delicious and Mother had a good time as well. There were little shops for her to browse in, an excellent dance orchestra to listen to, and all manner of dancing for her to watch.

She even found guests who spoke English. Our hotel manager was a relative of Victor Mature and had lived in the States for years, so she could talk about her beloved U.S.A.

One memory I especially treasure from that holiday. It had started to snow towards the end of the day, and I witnessed the startling but harmless collision on the slopes between a stoutish, middle-aged German and a little wisp of an Italian woman. How did I know their nationalities? To the delight of everyone, as they vanished down the slope doing a very intricate but un-planned ski routine, there came floating up to us a fine deep masculine *"Gott im Himmel,"* and a plaintive, anguished, and very feminine *"Mama mia, Mama mia!"*

Signor Bruno's message that we once more had running wa-ter coincided with a most wonderful snow storm, but we made it back safely in a world of white beauty. Our new water pipe went through Giovanni's farmyard, up over the fence and higher yet up through the fig trees. As well as being one of the smartest dressers I have ever seen, Signor B. was smart in a prac-tical way also. The pipe was just high enough to let a truck drive under it.

As the pipe was all above ground, a continuous flow of wa-ter was necessary to keep our water supply from freezing again. We attached a hose and kept it running to the edge of the lake. One particularly cold night, the stream of water was not suffi-cient and, oh horrors! It froze again. Kim drove off to work rue-fully as I set to work with the zeal of a madwoman to light fires all along the pipe and have water again.

Giovanni once more came to my rescue and produced from his barn the most amazing supply of combustible material, everything from corn cobs to palm fibre. We worked like beavers, and burned ourselves on the red hot pipe, but still no running water. Mother was stationed at her French door and was to give the signal when she heard water running in the bathroom. Finally, I had the idea of placing sheets of newspaper on the pipe where it arched up over the fence. As I lit these papers, I wondered what an engineer would think of my tactics, but those burning newspapers did the trick! Giovanni and I performed a dance of jubilation as once more the water ran through our pipe. You can be assured that there never was too small a trickle again.

But this flow of water may have been at least partly responsible for yet another *disastro*. One Monday morning, Kim had to go in to the *municipio* to fill out the endless forms and papers that were necessary for us to live in Italy. Dearly as we loved Italy, we found the red tape, the receipts, the stamps required for every receipt and legal paper, frustrating. It seemed to be carried too far, and was more than tiring. Home was on Kim's way back to work after this necessary session, so he dashed in for a bite of lunch. He dashed in just a bit too quickly and forgot to engage the parking brake. Suddenly, Mother, who was sitting where she had the perfect view of it, said, "Is that our car going into the lake?" It was. What was amazing was that, though there was not a person in sight, within ten minutes people were arriving by the ice and on the road, on foot, on bicycles. The Bogni family, who had a small plastic factory on the ground floor level of their house midway to Gropello, arrived in their car. They had been sitting down to lunch on the second floor level and had seen our car start to roll, squeeze between two poplar trees and start to sink where our hose had weakened the shore ice. Until now I had had a smiling acquaintance with the family as I passed their house on my way to shop. They proved themselves friends indeed. They knew of a crane in the district and set off to get it for us while we started a rescue operation for objects in our fast-sinking car. Kim had spent the weekend working on reports and I had been writing letters, so we set about retrieving our weekend's work. Kim sprawled through the back door of the car and handed out the papers to me and to our large supply of willing volunteers, who rushed up our outside stone steps to spread them out on the living room floor to dry.

As soon as lunch was over, those that could came back for the afternoon's entertainment. Quite a number of women walked down for the show. Even one baby in a carriage arrived. I supplied as much seating as I could, and even provided one hat. Norah had left a yellow ribbon hat for me to dispose of. I had felt sure some child could use it for dress up, and now that yellow hat added a real note of colour to the rather sombre clothing of the waiting audience. Italian women in our neighbourhood never wore overcoats, just a warm crocheted shawl cape, usually black or gray. Even babies wore those capes. I was always amazed that babies wore kerchiefs on their heads and did not pull them off. The baby who attended the extraction of our car was as good as gold.

When the great crane lumbered down our lane, followed by a jeep from our excellent garage (recommended by our good friend Angelo), everyone leaned forward in expectation. It was not long before our car was hoisted out and hung up there in the air for all the world like so many of the little perch we had seen dangling from fishing lines. I called out to Kim, "Get a picture of that." He said, "I thought of it myself, but you know I always carry the camera in the front of the car, ready for any good shots as I drive to work." The camera had been soaked, though we managed to salvage some pictures that had been on the film.

Our car was towed away to Varese, water "oozing from every pore," and our audience followed it up the lane. Such was the simple humour of many of our neighbours that they were delighted with Kim's explanation that he had felt it was time that the car had a wash. The car was back with us the next evening, running fine, but definitely humid and smelling faintly fishy.

The Bogni family had been so quick to come to our aid that I made a batch of cookies and invited them over the next evening. Alessandro worked with his father in the plastic factory. His sister, Luciana, was soon to marry the good friend he had made while away on military service. Silvana was still in grade school, and that evening I marvelled once more at how well-behaved an Italian child could be through hours of adult conversation. That evening we showed them slides of Canada. The slides, and what they called Canadian cookies, made a great impression on them. Italians almost always buy cakes when they are entertaining and are very impressed with home baking. Both the girls were exceptionally pretty. Mother was delighted with them, and with the handsome son. I had felt Signora Bogni to be, as the Italians say, *simpatica*, and now we had the pleasure of knowing the whole family.

Like ourselves, they were lovers of the outdoors, and we would often meet them walking or down around the lake. The next summer, Kim went fishing with Signor Bogni. One good result from our car bath was our friendship with this family.

Silvana must have spoken at school about the Kodachromes, for Carmella had heard of them, and arrived on the Saturday afternoon to ask if she could see one. It was a bright day, but Kim flashed a couple on the wall for her. She was very impressed and felt it would be both interesting and educational for her school to see them. She tried with all the energy of her nine years to organize it, but the staff of her school was not as enthusiastic as she was. We invited her and Enrico down on the Friday evening to see them. They were solemnly delivered to our door by their slim, shy father. After the pictures, they had a feed of their first toasted marshmallows and popcorn by our fireside. We could hear their voices in the still night as they went up the lane with their father, trying to tell him all they had seen, and just what marshmallows and popcorn tasted like. Right after lunch the next afternoon, their large mother arrived at our door with a small tin pail. She had walked down that cold day with just her shawl for warmth and had sandals on her feet. These are the thick wooden clogs the country folk wear. She insisted on leaving these outside for fear of dirtying the floor. In the tin pail were two eggs, her thank you for the pleasure we had given her beloved children. During this cold winter, the hens were laying so poorly I knew how precious those eggs were.

Chapter 9

Spring Brings Adventures
Further Afield

That winter of 1962-63 remained very cold, but the sunshine was brilliant.

One day, from the direction of Calcinate, came the fisherman, Antonio, and another man. When I saw it was Antonio, I knew it was some job for Signor Bruno, for Antonio was his employee and right-hand man. The project this time was to move the red tiles left over from our roof to a lakeside cabin that Signor Bruno was having built as a clubhouse and small restaurant for his summer water skiers. The tiles were carried down to the ice, piled on a ladder and then easily dragged back to the clubhouse on the ice. Once more my hat was off to Signor Bruno, for this was the quickest and easiest way of getting the tiles from our place to his. Numerous trips were made and the pile under our plum tree grew smaller and smaller. Sad to say, any tiles that broke were shot out onto our lovely ice.

Once more, Italians were living for the moment. Now we would have to retrieve those broken tiles, or look at them until the ice melted. Farther down the lake were broken bottles and pieces of wood. The Italians of all ages seemed to have a passion for shooting things out onto the frozen lake. Every piece hurt me aesthetically, for I delighted in that ice. I managed to avoid them all when I was skating, but poor Duke got a bad cut on one foot and gave up accompanying me up and down the lake.

Just as it was unusual to find an Italian like Signor Bruno, who would throw himself into so many types of work, so it was unusual to find a fisherman like Antonio, who would take on any job. While the ice remained frozen, most of the fishermen waited until they could fish again, fishing being their trade.

The local people told us that bundles of reeds were put down in the spring for fish to lay eggs on them. These canes rotted and a gas was created that made the ice unsafe. The locals insisted that, if you broke the ice you could light the bubbles of gas. I had already begun to feel maybe the ice was not so safe, and the stories of bubbles of gas convinced me it was time to hang up my borrowed skates.

During the rest of the winter, on the weekdays that I did not have to make shopping excursions, I would walk briskly to Calcinate and visit with Signora Zannetti in her cozy kitchen behind the *tabaccaio*. Her only son would be on duty in the shop, but her two married daughters were usually with her, as their shops were closed for the siesta time. Not only did I enjoy the company, but it was a language lesson for me as well. My ever-handy dictionary was constantly in use as I tried to follow their conversation and add a bit myself.

I often stayed until Giovanna, the little daughter of one of the sisters, came in from school, in her black smock with the bright bow of ribbon at her throat. She was an excellent student, and her books were a marvel of neatness for an eight-year-old. She was loved so wholeheartedly by her mother, her grandmother and her aunt, that there seemed no difference in her relationship with any of them.

Some days, I walked in the other direction and visited Signora Giamberini in her home behind the old wooden water wheel in Gropello. Before I reached her place, I passed the open laundry where, usually, two or three women would be scrubbing and talking. I was glad to see that, as a concession to that ice-cold water, they wore rubber gloves. Signora Giamberini was fortunate in that she had a small washing machine and running water in the house. In summer, she washed outside in her own private tub beside the big old water wheel.

She was well known in the district as a very competent seamstress. When I visited her that winter, she had two young girls, about fourteen years of age, whom she was teaching to sew. It was as though they were apprenticed. The one girl had been born with two club feet, and nothing had been done to correct the deformity. Signora Gamberini had the greatest compassion for her but insisted that each sewing assignment be done well, or it was ripped out and done again. I felt I should not intrude into these sewing sessions, but the Signora told me they would be happy to have me drop in every day.

Hospitality was such a rite that out would come the little silver tray and small glasses, and we four had to have a drink. The girls had just a token drink, but they were always included.

As I made these walks to and fro, I missed the lizards' quick darting in the grass beside the road. At first it used to startle me, and now that they were hibernating, I missed them.

Often the afternoons would find me climbing the hill to the Bottini's villa. With my dictionary and my sewing, I would join the Signora by her open fire in the smaller living room. She was always knitting something in black and very stylish. Even without Italian, we had become dear friends, and as my Italian improved, the bond between us grew stronger. Oh, how lucky we were to have the Bottinis for neighbours. The family who had the summer place just beside us on the lake came often to their house but kept completely to themselves.

If Giannina in her kitchen saw me pass on my way to visit the Signora, she would beam at me, for she loved her beloved mistress to have company. The Signora and Giannina were almost like sisters. Giannina was a very intelligent woman who was loved and deeply respected by the whole Bottini family. She had a second son, Gianfranco, when she was older, and I knew that the Signora had often given him his noon meal, so that Giannina might slip away for a much needed nap. Kim and I used to tell the Signora she was an "Angela" by name and an angel by nature. She stoutly denied such goodness.

When our relationship was such that she called me *"tesoro,"* treasure, or *"stella,"* star, the tears came to my eyes. These are terms of endearment in Italian, and how I treasured them. I had now so completely entered into the Italian way of life that even the quick Italian tears came whenever I was moved.

That winter of 1962-63 was said to be the coldest since 1927, and many said it was the coldest ever. We were told that it had done more damage to very old buildings than the past two thousand years had done. Severe as the cold was, Giovanni and the local farmers managed to produce fresh greens from under the mats they had woven from the rushes and placed to catch as much sunshine as possible. The salad greens amazed and delighted Kim and me as there were eleven varieties, and many we had never tasted before. These salad greens appeared only during the winter months.

Despite the intense cold, no overcoats appeared locally. The women put on an extra skirt and had a thicker, intricately knitted shawl for the shoulders. In the cities, there were baby carriages, but in the country, babies were usually held in a pair of loving arms. Often, I marveled at the strength of older arms that could manage a beloved grandchild and a basket of groceries as well.

As a lift to everyone's spirits, along came *Carnevale*. There is celebration and a feeling of excitement before Lent, since in Italy, and the Italian canton of Switzerland, there is *Carnevale*. The "*vale*" in medieval Latin means "farewell" and the "*carne*" is meat, so we have "farewell to meat" for Lent. Hence, also, our word "carnival."

At this time the stores had costumes for sale, but many costumes were lovingly and lavishly made at home. The week before, fond and doting parents parade their children in attractive costumes. During the day of *Carnivale*, the children throw confetti and streamers and have all kinds of noise makers and balloons. In the evenings, the adults have merry parties. I frequently saw adults in costume on the day as well. Each place seemed to have a special day for celebration, so for over a week we saw costumes and enjoyed the feeling of excitement in the air.

Milan observes the Gregorian calendar, which runs two weeks later than the Julian calendar that is in common use. We were out for a Sunday drive after we thought all the festivities were over, and quite unexpectedly got caught up in a *Carnivale* procession that was adhering to the Gregorian calendar. There were small floats, *papier maché* figures with bobbing heads, both lovely and grotesque. It was a small parade, but it really played havoc with the Sunday afternoon traffic in Milan.

In some parts of Italy, especially those by the sea, these processions are very sumptuous and magnificent. The celebration is called *Mardi Gras*, "Tuesday fat," a feast to use up all cooking fat before Lent begins. It is the origin of our Pancake Tuesday.

In our village of Calcinate, the school children celebrate gaily but with little expense. The school supplied brightly coloured paper hats and skirts and capes. Fortunately, it was a bright, warm day as the colourful procession of children wound down the road from Upper Calcinate to the *cooperativo*. Every child was blowing a paper horn festooned with ribbons. As well as its store, every *cooperativo* has a large room where the men can have a drink, and on Saturday nights play cards. This day the large room had been cleared of tables. The children poured in, blowing on their horns. When they had assembled, their teacher, a woman of ample proportions, stood on a box and led the children in singing. I was amazed by the quality and beauty of their singing. Their loving and proud parents, mothers only as the men were at work, beamed approval.

Bruna made sure that I missed nothing. I do not know who supplied the children with their cookies and drinks. Only the children had refreshments, and they had a marvelous time. We moved outside, where the men play *Botte*, a game of bowls. A photographer was taking advantage of the sunshine and getting pictures of the children in their paper finery. Since the school had no organized parent groups, the mothers had no responsibility for costumes or refreshments.

As the days went by, there came a spell of misty rain, and in three days the ice was gone from the lake. The fishermen were back on the lake in their crescent-shaped boats. I watched them row from a standing position amidships, and saw they had lost none of their skill during their enforced rest.

In no time, patches of ground were white with blossoms of *bucaneve*, an Italian name for "snowdrops" meaning, literally, "hole in the snow." Spring came in a rush. Soon the walk up the lane was edged with violets and the banks of the stream were golden with primroses. I had feared for the fruit trees during the cold, but instead of being harmed, the trees seemed to have benefited, bursting into an absolute frenzy of blossom. I had never seen apricot trees in bloom and I was thrilled with the delicate blossoms.

With all that land about our home, my old gardening instinct became too strong. I just had to have a garden too. The land should really have been ploughed, but Giovanni found us a willing man, expert with a shovel. He turned up early in the mornings to dig before he went off to his regular job. Anyone seeing the energy he put into that digging would be ready ever afterwards to challenge any labeling of "lazy Italians." Kim and I knew how heavy that soil was and marveled that he could achieve such a beautifully turned over garden for us.

Despite my assuring Giovanni that I always planted my own garden, he would not allow it. It was not the work for a Signora. Beds were prepared and planted in the Italian way. Lettuce, radish, and carrot seeds were planted, not in rows, but broadcast over a plot small enough to be reached from all sides. Since I had never planted *zuccini*, he did allow me to plant those.

Flower planting could be a woman's work, so here I thought I was on my own, but Signor Bruno turned up with very definite ideas about flower planting. As he had such good taste, I followed his suggestions. I am not sure that I was strong enough to oppose him in any event. Later, we enjoyed the product of his ideas. Mother loved the vivid colour of zinnias, so I put them all down the drive where she could enjoy them from her room, and even from her bed.

Never have I had such a vegetable garden. The Italian sun took over. Picking my green peas presented quite a problem, for they grew over six feet tall.

During our stay in Italy, of the sixteen days set aside as holidays, eleven had religious significance. St. Joseph's Day, March 19, was one of these holy days, and it fell on a Tuesday. This meant we had what was known at Ispra as a "bridge" weekend. Monday could be taken as a holiday and paid for later by a day's work on a Saturday.

With four free days, we set off to explore Verona. I had studied our Guide Bleu and knew that among the cities of Venetia, it is second only to Venice for the interest of its monuments, and that it is especially noted for the quality of its Roman ruins. We were blessed with a fine clear day and made such good time on the autostrada that we arrived by lunch time. The glowing accounts of the city had me expecting all the beauty of the Taj Mahal. Verona had been bombed, and much of the beauty I was expecting was not there. We found the beauty later, but I had been carried away by the guidebook and had over-anticipated.

Unbeknownst to us, a big, agricultural fair is always held in Verona at this time. It was St. Joseph's weekend, and we discovered that there was no room at any hotel for us. What was bitter disappointment at the time turned out to be wonderful luck. After many inquiries, one most obliging hotel manager found accommodation for us in a country hotel, "La Vela d'Oro," the Golden Sail. It was about a fifteen-minute drive from Verona, and right on the shore of Italy's largest lake, Lago di Garda. Since a place to put our heads for the night was of prime importance, we set forth immediately after our lunch, eaten in a charming little restaurant on a quiet back street, also recommended by our hotel manager.

We drove out into the country, dark green with cypress-covered hills and silvery green with olive trees. We passed the peach and cherry orchards Verona is famous for. As we came nearer to the lake, every bit of land was growing grapes. We knew this district was renowned for its wines, Bardolino and Valpolicella. I remembered back in Canada seeing the name Lazise on the label of bottles of Italian wine, so that when suddenly we came upon this old walled town, we had to take time to drive through the gate in its medieval wall. A great part of this impressive wall still encloses the town, as it did in the days of its former importance when the overlords of Verona held court there. It is now a very quiet fishing village that has fine vineyards on the slopes around it. The old castle looked so fascinating we knew we would have to come back and explore it.

Our Vela d'Oro was a few miles farther along the shore, and when we had Mother comfortably settled for a siesta, we set forth to explore the beauty of the lake. The water of Garda is a beautiful blue and clear, clear. The dark green of the cypress and the silver green of the olive trees had gone to our heads. We could not decide whether the silver green was a haze, a mist or a faint smoke. Our hotel manager had told us an Englishman by the name of "Wash," (which we felt sure must be "Walsh") had a delightful villa overlooking the lake, so we let that be our goal. We left the car by the roadside, and walked in through lovely grounds to the villa.

It was an old villa, four hundred years old, and a beauty. Mr. Wash, or Walsh, was not there, but we could look in the windows and see the part he occupied. There were a number of workmen around who pointed out special features to us. Our hearts were warmed by their friendliness and kindness.

It was coming on to that peaceful time just before twilight as we started our walk back through the grounds to the car. There is an atmosphere you can feel when a garden has been a garden for so long. The shoreline was picturesque with rugged rocks, the lake was lapping so softly it was just breaking against the shore, and no more. Every olive tree we passed entranced us. The road from the villa was lined with great conical cypresses. There was such beauty about us that it all had a dreamlike quality. I truly wondered if I could be dreaming when down the avenue towards us came an ancient, vintage car. It was painted a soft yellow, and strapped on the roof was a marvelous old hat box. Kim and I were transfixed with delight for we have a weakness for old cars, and it was a beauty. Then we saw that it was being used as an advertising stunt, for painted on the side was a bottle of Ramazzoti, one of those bitter, herbal drinks which flourish in Italy. The mellow old bulbous horn was honked at us. Two men in the car had all the charm and winning grace of Italians. We were gallantly presented with miniature bottles of Ramazzotti.

Kim and I returned to our hotel in a daze. We had experienced such beauty and there was something magical about that fine old car driving up the avenue of trees. La Vela d'Oro found it did not pay to keep its restaurant open except in the summer. The manager directed us to a little restaurant in the village of Bardolino, on the shore of Lake Garda. He assured us that the food was superb and, as he said it, he had a look savouring past feasts.

Before we set off, I read in our guide book: "Bardolino, famous for red wine, a few traces of ramparts and some Renaissance houses, in the main square, church of 11th century..." When there is so much beauty and atmosphere in Italy, how can they prepare you for the charm of these small fishing harbour towns? We took this place to our hearts. It was not just cupboard love, although the meal we had that night in the Bardolino Hotel was one of the best we had ever eaten, and Italy had been treating us royally. The kitchen door was, and always is, open, so you see your fish being placed over the hot coals or your meat being grilled. The cooks are older, generously proportioned women and they are charming. There were young waitresses instead of waiters. In this district where the grape, the olive and fish are the main products, the men have enough to do without being waiters. The food was all you could imagine food could be, but the simple surroundings and friendly atmosphere were just as pleasing.

We fell completely under the spell of this place and, during our stay in Italy, visited whenever we could. We felt so at home at the Hotel Bardolino that we had to resist the temptation on a Saturday to drive over for a meal. Later we saw our restaurant written up in the "Gastronomic Delights of Italy" and were thrilled to see the picture of the two women cooking over the large old wood stove and the faces of our friendly young waitresses. We lingered long at our table that first night, enjoying the pleasure of the people about us as they enjoyed their food.

We found Verona the perfect city for sightseeing with Mother, as it was possible to get the car close to all the places of interest. We visited the arena first. We knew that it is second only to Rome in size, but were quite unprepared for its fine condition. It is used every summer for opera and must have had considerable repair work done on it, as it was built in 290 A.D. but the work has been done so cleverly that it in no way jars. It will seat an audience of twenty-five thousand.

There were many tiers of steps to climb for the view from the top, but I made it. I was so proud of myself that I went and bought a postcard of the arena and sent it to my optometrist in Canada. When I had got my bifocals, I found stairs quite difficult to manage and ventured a mild complaint to him. He turned on me, and in a rather withering tone said, "ninety percent of the world can adjust to bifocals, but of course you might be one of the ten percent who can't." My reaction had been defiant, and all I put on the card was "I have just made all these steps, so you see I am one of the ninety percent."

We visited Juliet's house. The balcony was much lower and smaller than I had been led to expect from all the movies and plays I had seen of this tragic love story. There, over the archway into the courtyard, is a carved hat, crest of her family, the Capulets. Down the street, and around the corner, we found the house where Romeo was reputed to have lived.

We saw the exquisite Roman theatre some lucky archeologists had the joy of excavating. We drove over the bridge Caesar had crossed to conquer Gaul. All my early disappointment in Verona was gone as we leisurely explored. We wandered around the *Piazza dell'Erbe* (grass market) with all its little stalls and umbrellas and awnings. As I looked at all the picturesque fruit, flowers and vegetable stands, I tried to imagine the days this spot had been a Roman forum and chariot races had been held right where we were standing. An Italian passerby, who could see our interest in everything, pointed out to us where the moneylenders, like Shylock, had lived and carried on their trade. He also told us to watch out for the little ladders in the wrought ironwork adorning the unusual tombs of the famous Scaligere family. These tombs are above ground and very ornate. One of the princesses of this family married into a noble Milanese family and is buried in a little chapel under the La Scala opera house. It is from the emblem of the Scaligere family that La Scala received its name. *Scala* means "ladder." There, in Verona, the elaborate ironwork on the tombs contained many small ladders cleverly worked into the design.

Mother particularly enjoyed strolling along the Via Mazzini, lined with very attractive shops, guaranteed to part you from some of your money. No traffic is allowed here so there is nothing to distract you from the merchandise, so enticingly displayed. The somber elegance of the Piazza dei Signori we found most impressive. We were delighted that the statue of Dante could look so dignified, even with his head adorned with live pigeons. I really do not like pigeons, but such a dear old lady was selling spills of dried corn that I bought some and joined a group of children to feed the pigeons.

A short distance from this square, we went up five pink marble steps under an arch and into the charming Piazza Massante. There we admired the old pink marble well and an outside staircase that must be one of the treasures of all Europe.

By now I wondered how I could possibly have been disappointed in Verona. It is an intimate city and you are able to comprehend all its beauty and hold it to you. Fortunately for us, almost everyone must have been at the Fair, for many times we had these spots to ourselves.

Even with frequent rests, Mother was tired, so we left her in the car outside the church of St. Zeno Maggiore, one of the finest Romanesque churches in Northern Italy. So far as we could find out, St. Zeno is the only negro who was canonized. He lived in 300 A.D. and, as I looked at his saintly face in the great statue in red marble, I wondered how this African had come to be the patron saint of Verona.

Late afternoon found us sitting out in the sunshine in an outdoor café in the piazza, having coffee and the golden cake that is the specialty of Verona. We were watching people, a most popular pastime in Italy, and enjoying the fine cedar trees in the central garden when, to our delight, up drove our vintage car of yesterday. We were greeted like old friends. This time we had our camera and were able to get pictures. Now Mother could understand our enthusiasm of yesterday.

We went back to Bardolino for dinner, only twenty minutes' drive from the center of Verona. Once more there were several groups of men enjoying their meal and each other's company. I wondered what the women in their lives were doing while they were having dinner and such a good time.

That night we had *vitello Bolognese,* and it was even better than we had eaten in Bologna. This dish has a slice of veal, a slice of ham and cheese melted on top, and that night the whole thing melted in our mouths. We were so delighted with our Saturday and Sunday dinners that we turned up for breakfast Monday morning. This was a mistake. The Hotel Bardolino did not cater for breakfasts. Wonderful dinners and mid-day meals they could and did produce, but even the staff breakfasted at home. However, the waitresses were as charming and friendly as ever. They were busy bringing in what I thought were yellow curtains and spreading them carefully over the tables. The yellow curtains turned out to be the freshly made dough foundation that would appear in the noon pasta of lasagna.

We could not stay to sample it, for Kim had a surprise for us. He had planned, if the weather was good and Mother felt up to more driving, to go on up to Merano to see if it measured up to Bimbi and Reinier's glowing accounts. Even if there had been no pot of gold at the end of the trip, the drive in itself was a joy. Lago di Garda is truly a beautiful lake. We drove along the east shore for miles with the blue, blue water on our left and a majestic mountain range of grey rock on our right, often rising so steeply up from the water that we were frequently driving in and out of tunnels. The dark green cypress rose up everywhere, and wherever there was tillable soil, there were vineyards or olive trees. Many times we saw healthy, brown-faced women kneeling at the lake's edge on their little wooden wash platforms. I saw one pause to brush a strand of hair away from her face, and as her eyes looked out over the lake, I thought what a view to have while doing washing. Every time that my eyes travelled up to a high rocky point that seemed completely inaccessible, there would be either a church or the remains of an old castle. It is a mystery to me how they got their building supplies up to these high peaks.

The mountains at the northern end of the lake rose steeply and straight from the water's edge. After driving a climbing zigzag road for a short distance, and then through a pass, the scenery completely changed. A plateau opened up and there were miles and miles of apple orchards. I knew that apples came from this region because in the autumn, to my great surprise, I had been able to buy apples cheaper than I could in Canada.

As we drove on, we saw that men and young boys were wearing aprons, dark green or blue, and wore Tyrolean hats. Some men, striding along the roadside or driving flocks of sheep, wore graceful black capes. Then slogans began to appear on rock faces. The district around Bolzano had been Austrian before the Great War of 1914-1918. During the last war, sympathies had been with the Germans. The region speaks German as well as Italian, and there were those – particularly young men – who wanted it returned to Austria. Now, every railroad station and every bridge was guarded by soldiers from Italian regiments. Later, when we would read of a bridge being blown up or a road worker being killed by a bomb blast, it would seem so much more immediate to us.

In our district of Varese, statues of Christ were in glass cases with artificial flowers arranged at the foot of the cross. Up here, the Christ hung on a wooden cross with a wooden shingle roof for protection and often a few fresh mountain leaves at the foot of the cross. As we neared Bolzano, we began to see high-peaked church roofs of shiny green tiles arranged in interesting designs.

Then we entered the valley leading to Merano, and we saw that all that Bimbi and Reinier had told us was true. There were castles everywhere. The mountains were beautiful. Vineyards covered the lower slopes. Here the beauty was not stark and rugged, but peaceful. The town was picturesque and charming. As we drove up the main street, we spied Bimbi and Reinier swinging along with a shopping basket between them. We had an excited meeting and followed them to the home of Bimbi's mother. While we had tea by the fireside, a phone call was made for us, and in no time we had rooms with a family friend.

Merano is such a beautiful spot and so popular that, in spite of the many hotels, anyone who has rooms takes in guests. The home where we stayed was very large. It had been built by a group of dry goods merchants as a retirement home. Now it was privately owned and the ground floor made a perfect guest house while our host lived on the second floor.

The charm of Merano is such that, once you have visited it, you have to go back. You become an "ancient mariner" holding people by the lapels with your tale of its beauty and atmosphere. You look up at the high mountains all around and you always hear water running. The river Adige flows through the city (and later through the city of Verona). The local landowners all have water runways through their properties. At certain times the sluices are opened, and the water comes gushing through the drainage ditches or canals.

I believe there are 189 castles in the district, and even fairyland could not have castles more picturesque. There is a strong Austrian atmosphere, especially in the charming restaurants. Some of these are on the second floors of buildings and overlook the river. Others are under arcades or on the far side of courtyards. Many of the streets have shops under the covered archways. It is customary to go out for dinner, and that evening we met many delightful and unusual people. I wish I could share the tales and fascinating snippets of gossip I have heard in Merano. The South Tyrol shares the Austrian fascination with human foibles and eccentricities. Ezra Pound spent much of his life here. Then there was Madame Burg, whom we met on a later visit, who had been wooed and won by a member of the Hapsburg family. The marriage was frowned upon by senior members of the family, and when her husband died, the family gave her the very elegant hunting lodge in Merano as a residence but would not allow her to use the Hapsburg name. She became Madame Burg.

During our visit, people were full of the story of one of the more prominent young men whose mother detested the piano. She would not allow her son to have one in the castle. He had a piano completely disassembled and reassembled in a remote tower of the castle where he could play it without his mother's hearing it.

We had literally to tear ourselves away the next morning, we had so completely fallen under the spell of Merano, but we knew we would be back.

We drove, this time, down the western shore of Lago di Garda, where the mountains rise straight up from the lake edge. The many tunnels in this road were used during the war for safe storage of critical heavy machinery. We would suddenly come out of a tunnel into brilliant sunshine, and there would be a settlement squeezed between the mountain and the lake. We were surprised to find the local people selling oranges and lemons with clusters of shiny dark green leaves, so shiny they seemed waxed. When we stopped for lunch, with a magnificent view of the fifty kilometer-long lake, we found that, since the district, "Limone," has a milder climate, regulated by the lake, and has protection from the north winds, these fruits can be grown this far north. It is rather a complicated business, for some protection has to be provided. You might call them "lemon houses," wooden structures for protection in winter. The lemons and sweet oranges are grafted onto a native bitter orange because plants raised from seed are prey to disease. St. Francis of Assisi, who came to Garda and founded a church and monastery, is reputed to have brought the lemon. The old church of San Francesco, in its cloisters, has ancient and beautiful carvings of leaves and fruit upon the pillars, so perhaps this is true. The local people claim their lemons have "double the strength of ordinary lemons." As to the truth of this I cannot say, but they do have an exquisite fragrance, and what a splash of colour they make as you drive out of one of those dark tunnels.

When we finally drove down our lane that night, it seemed incredible that we had seen so much and only been away four days.

We had barely settled down to our quiet life by our peaceful lake when Kim found that he must go to Bologna again. It was apple blossom time, so we decided to take a few more days of our holidays and go by way of Merano and Venice. The drive along the length of Lago di Garda was as thrilling as ever. The grapevines were growing up the hillsides. Then, suddenly, we would come upon a little bay with fishnets spread out to dry.

We had our lunch in the Bardolino Hotel, first looking in the open kitchen door and being greeted by all, although this was only the fourth time they had seen us. We drank a particularly good wine and Kim was eager to buy us a supply of it. The proprietor guided us through a few, twisting, narrow streets to a marvelous old wine cellar. The barrels were so large that you could imagine setting up housekeeping in one of them. This was our first visit to such a place, and I do not think we missed anything. You certainly could not miss the smell of fermentation. It lingered on my clothes even when we were back out of the darkness and in the bright sunlight again. Once the bottles were safely packed away in the trunk of our car, Kim asked how much we owed. The proprietor said, "Next time you come, I will have your bill ready for you." We knew the food of his famous kitchen would lure us back, but felt honoured by his trust. We had never before received this treatment from a comparative stranger. We drove on up to Merano in a warm glow of pleasure.

Sad to say, the apple blossoms were past their prime but were lovely in a fragile way. Once more, when we got up into the mountain country, I was thrilled by the flowing cloaks many of the men wore. Not only are these cloaks picturesque, but they must be very practical with all that extra material to provide warmth.

It is amazing the way the landscape in Italy can change so quickly. The houses, too, will be quite different. Even the dress changes. As soon as we left Lago di Garda, the olive and cypress gave way to vineyards and fruit trees, and the great villas by the lake were replaced with squat, very utilitarian farm dwellings. Then soon there would be men and boys in their aprons, usually a lovely blue.

In Merano, it was so warm the women were wearing gay cotton dresses with different types of aprons over them, held with silver clasps, no apron ties. The men were wearing Tyrolean costumes with bright hats and knickers, and their ties were held by a handsome silver clasp. If unmarried, they wore a red tie, and if married, green.

Quite by chance, we had come to Merano during a festival of village bands. We arrived as the parade of bands began. The Tyrolean costumes on the girls and young women were lovely. Aprons were beautifully embroidered. There were some young women with very intricate head ornaments of fine silver and some dashing hats with swooping feathers.

Almost every band was led by a small boy, carrying a plaque showing the name of the village, very conscious of the importance of his job. Then a bevy of lovely girls in costume followed, carrying flowers or little wooden liqueur barrels. Then came the bands, with their instruments polished to the last degree. Many of the older men had fine mountain faces. Everyone looked so healthy and happy.

Mother was in seventh heaven, for she loved a band. We found her a bench, and I found myself a fountain no longer in use and stood in it to get a better view. Kim was almost desperate, snapping pictures right and left, trying to capture as much of the colour and gaiety as he could. Some of the girls were beautiful, and we have many pictures of them. I stood in my dry fountain and wept for sheer happiness at the colour, the gaiety and the music.

In the evening, the competitors assembled in a huge hall. We bought tickets stamped out of metal, showing a man in Tyrolean costume playing the cymbals. We sat around at tables and ate and drank while we listened to bands. Sometimes part of a band would be up in the balcony. It was beautiful to hear the melody being answered from above. A band from Holland won first prize that evening. The Dutch conductor, who accepted the prize, spoke good German and brought the house down in laughter when he said,"God made the earth in six days, and if he had one more day he would have made it all flat like Holland." The local people knew how the Dutch love the mountains, and this delighted them.

Walking back from parking our car after the concert, we met Madame Burg, whom we had met on our earlier visit. She invited us to tea at her home the next afternoon. Her home was a hunting lodge rather than a castle, but it was on a grand scale. As we had tea, Mother, with her love of antiques, was everywhere. There was a case of jeweled birds, miraculously made so they all moved and sang, and a fabulous clock with a music box built into it. As in buildings of a former era, there were no halls; one room opened into the next. Somehow, pictures of Napoleon's wives and paintings and photographs of the Hapsburgs meant so much more to us when we knew they were family portraits. The quaint old tiled stoves particularly delighted Kim and me.

There were two never-to-be-forgotten incidents that weekend. One was going into an old cathedral to find it full of the music of the organ and accompanying wind instruments. The other was of waking at daybreak to the sound of horn music floating down the mountainside. Some player had gone up there to practice, or to welcome the day.

The drive from Merano to Venice was impressive. Much of the time we were following fast-flowing streams. We had a delicious trout from one of these streams for our lunch. We were parking our car by the ferry for Venice by mid-afternoon. Marguerita, one of our skiing friends from Madonna di Campiglio, had parents who owned a hotel on the Lido. We had decided to stay there and share some family life. We enjoyed our close association with Marguerita and her family, but it was a mistake as far as sightseeing was concerned, for we spent so much time on the ferry coming and going.

Seeing Venice was a dream come true for me, and everything lived up to my expectations. The beauty and atmosphere were beyond anything I had expected. There was such perfection in the buildings that, even where one couldn't see, the detail of the stonework around the windows was just as beautiful and perfect as on the imposing front. The builders of Venice were artists.

I loved the lapping water and the gently bobbing gondolas. The gondola is said to be of Turkish origin. They are built in Venice of oak, cherry, elm, walnut or pine. They are so well adapted to the needs of the city that there are only two places, even at the lowest tide, where they cannot pass. They are thirty-six feet long and have a beam of five feet. They are deliberately lopsided to counter the weight of the gondolier. Every three weeks in summer, they must be brought ashore, scraped of weeds and tarred again. Fares have to be high, as the gondoliers are largely unemployed in the winter months. It is not easy to scull a gondola, and the reverse stroke is almost as laborious as the forward stroke. When the boat approaches a corner, there are a series of warning cries, and there is a gliding motion involved in maneuvering the corner. The gondolier uses the footwork of a ballet dancer to accomplish the maneuver.

Marguerita, told us that the gondolas had all been painted black after a terrible plague in the sixteenthth century. It was she who pointed out to us that in the painting above the door of St. Mark's cathedral, St. Mark's body was hidden in a container of pork to protect it from the marauding Turks until it could be spirited away. You can see all the people in the painting holding their noses to avoid smelling the obnoxious pork.

She told us of special places to eat where we had marvelous seafood. Going about Venice with her, we saw so many things we might have missed on our own. Mother bought me some fine Murano glass, and I was surprised and delighted to have it packed in a box from E.D. Smith's, Winona, Ontario, Canada. Cousins of ours have a fruit farm right next door.

The first time we were sitting in a cafe on the St. Mark Piazza, enjoying the music being played first by one cafe orchestra and then another, Kim complained about the outrageously high price of his aperitif, and said he could get it for a fifth of the price at home. The waiter told us they paid fifty thousand lire a month just to have a spot on the Piazza, and that if Kim went around to the next street he could get his drink at the price he was accustomed to paying. He showed a fine sense of humour in telling us this. One of the other waiters was rather slow and our waiter slipped in behind him and gave a dumb show of cranking him up.

We were lucky to enjoy Venice in the spring, for I understand many find it crowded and even smelly later in the summer. We had to tear ourselves away and head for Bologna, where business went well for Kim. Once more, we were wined and dined in the famous Bolognese manner. We were even more pleased with the city than before.

It was pretty late as we drove into Varese, and we stopped at the Hotel Europa to let Mother make use of the downstairs bathroom. She came back almost helpless with laughter. It seemed that an Italian man was on his way into the bathroom as she was coming out. He was unbuttoning his fly (no zippers in men's suits in Italy, as tailors feel they spoil the line of the suit). With one hand busy with his fly, he gallantly held the door open for Mother with his other hand. Doggerel always came easy to Mother, and when she stopped laughing, she gave us " Italian Courtesy":

> One hand was on the doorknob,
> The other on his fly;

But he bowed and smiled politely,
As he moved to let me by.

One day early in April the sun blazed forth and brought a breathtaking surprise. The fields around us were just crimson with poppies, thousands of them. We ate our breakfast on the balcony that morning hardly able to take our eyes from the fields.

Chapter 10

More Visitors and a Country Wedding

That spring we were saddened by the illness and death of Pope John. He was deeply loved, and the Italians affectionately called him "Johnny Walker," as he was such a great traveller. Everyone seemed depressed, and the weather was dull, overcast and rainy for weeks. Somehow it reminded me of the weather that so often comes on Good Friday. People even spoke in quieter voices. It was a pensive, reflective time. I realized one of Giovanni's cows was with calf, for I had read once that "Flan O'Brien said he loved the moo of the pregnant cow." It is a special moo, and now I knew why he loved it. That moo was the perfect accompaniment for these sad, expectant days.

In May, the youngest of my sisters, Samena, and her friend, Peg, visited us at the lake. Since it was their first trip abroad (they still had young families), we met them at the airport with sprays of red roses to make their arrival more special. It was a crystal clear day, and they arrived with eyes still full of wonder at the magnificent views over the Alps. Malpensa, Milan's international airport, is in Gallarate, a manufacturing town, but we knew all the attractive squares and picturesque buildings to drive past.

Once out in the country, they were exclaiming over old church spires and red-tiled farm buildings clustered on a hillside, and everywhere the bursting green of an Italian spring. They were taking in so much so suddenly, that I heard one say, "Look, a chicken." It had all the simplicity of a child finding an old friend. The day was so brilliantly clear that all our mountains were out to welcome them.

We drew off the road as it passed the end of our lake to give them an unforgettable, panoramic view. The snowy chain of the Alps to the west and north, dominated by the great massif of Monte Rosa, the sparkling lake, and Varese spread at the foot of our local mountain, Campo dei Fiori. Their whole visit was to be blessed with good weather. Spring flowers were in bloom in such profusion that it was breathtaking. The rhododendrons with their fountains of magnificent blossoms had them spellbound, as did the wisteria blossoms lifting in the faint breeze.

Everything happened just right for them. On their trip to Isola Bella, one of the white peacocks spread his tail to its full splendour for Samena's camera, and then followed her up the tiered garden to pose on one of the huge stone horses.

One day, when we were ready to walk up the lane to take the bus into Varese to shop for shirts for their husbands, Signor Bruno chanced to drive up, looking like a fashion plate. Not only did he drive us into town, but, since we were a bit early for the shop openings, he treated us to coffee in the piazza, introduced the girls to the owner of the most fashionable men's store in Varese and arranged a discount for them.

We treated them to dinner at our beloved Albergo Europa. It was the night Signora Stabalini's handsome son was home from Africa to visit his mother. He spoke English well, so we were able to find out much about Africa, and what a successful young Italian businessman felt about Italy and his adopted country.

After we visited the splendor of La Scala in Milan, we met Tina, the Bottini's daughter, who took us on a lightning tour of Milan that would be possible only with someone who knew and loved the city. We were in and out of fabulous offices that had lovely gardens at the back, with fountains and water gently dripping down onto mossy green stones. Then out into the street again. There is a much quicker pace of life in Milan. The Romans, who live at a slower pace, call a man who can't relax a Milanese.

Tina did not let us relax that morning. We went along streets where the simple, seventeenth century facades of buildings played down the wealth of the owners, who had not wanted to be targeted for taxes or for plunder. One of these buildings, a palace, we could enter because friends of Tina's worked in the very posh antique shop that rented a few rooms. The magnificence of the ceilings gave me a stiff neck, as I could not resist looking up. Here again there was an oasis of quietness in the cool garden and gentle fountain in an inner courtyard.

For lunch, Tina guided us to a restaurant seething with activity. Samena and Peg had almost as much pleasure in studying the elaborate menu as in the food. Our luncheon conversation was about Milan.

The Milanese are said to be the sharpest bargainers in all Italy. Their city is the capital of Lombardy, which has one-seventh of the land of Italy and, at that time, one-twelfth of the population, yet produced one-quarter of the country's income. The Milanese were complaining that they worked hard only to have money drained off to support the idlers of the South. The South were saying,"You in the North do not pay enough taxes." The North does need the labour of the many Southerners who flock north to find jobs. I was surprised to find that, until 1960, it was illegal to migrate from one part of the country to another. I then understood why each district had such different and distinctive customs and foods.

You have the feeling that the Milanese love money for what it can do. They spend it on cars, shops and art galleries. There is lavish spending on paintings and antique furniture. In Milan, they boast that the shops in the rest of Italy are stocked to please the tourist, but in Milan it is to please the Milanese.

Husbands in Milan really show off their wives with the money they spend on them. Gowns are gorgeous, and there is a profusion of jewels. Many people who are unable to get tickets for La Scala go simply to watch the magnificent procession of women entering the theatre. One is immediately conscious of the beauty and size of the diamonds worn by many Italian women, but the Milanese seem to surpass them all.

Tina saw to it that we caught the faster tempo of life, were conscious of the great wealth and saw some of the social life of Milan. Since she had a car, Peg and Samena were two of my guests who could visit Leonardo da Vinci's "Last Supper," to marvel that it was left untouched, when everything around it was destroyed by bombs. The trip to the Castello Sforzescho was most interesting with Tina as a guide, as there are paintings and sculptures that she loved so dearly that she had frequently skipped school to spend more time with them. Full as our day had been, there was time before we caught our train to sit at a sidewalk cafe and eat the famous Milan ice cream.

Since Peg and Samena were going by train to meet Peg's brother in Paris, I was determined they should see Berne, in Switzerland, on the way. I love the quaint beauty of that city, with its interesting fountains and famous clocks. I just had to be with Samena when she enjoyed them, so I left Kim and Mother and travelled to Switzerland with them.

There were no porters at either of the Varese stations. Then a dear, little, old and very courtly, gentleman insisted on helping them with their huge suitcases. It seems that most Italians, when they hear it is your first visit, have to ask if you find Italy beautiful. This dear old charmer spoke English so the girls could let him know just how enthusiastic they were about *la bella Italia*.

We had to change trains at Gavirate, and I initiated them into the Italian way of passing the suitcases out of the window rather than bumping down the corridor with them. Our tiny, eager friend nearly came out the window with the cases, but he was attentive and courtly to the end.

On the station platform, Samena and I enjoyed one of the best fits of giggles we have ever had. There were cases of small live pigs, and one pig either was not comfortable or had an emotional problem, for periodically he would go off into a high pig squeal that set all the others off. Everything would quiet down and we would begin to enjoy the flowers that seem a part of every Italian station, when our young troublemaker would start up again. Sam and I were so weak with laughter we could hardly climb onto the train. It was not that we were hard-hearted as to the plight of the piglets, it was just that the noise was so wild.

It was a joy travelling with these two, for they were so interested and enthusiastic about everything. Their delight in seeing Lago Maggiore and the islands again, their pleasure in the clear mountain streams and the painted mountain houses, the shapes of the roofs, all this had me glowing with pleasure. We had the compartment to ourselves and had our picnic of *cestini* lunches we had bought as we leaned out of the train window at Domodossola. The girls were delighted with the friendly vendor and his pushcart with the lunch bags and bottles of wine swinging in their raffia wrappings.

They were delighted with Berne. The weather was perfect. All window sills were gay with bright red geraniums.

I had to leave Peg and Samena to get back for my first Italian wedding, but I made sure that they knew of all the interesting and unusual restaurants in Berne.

We were amazed at the crowd of Italian men leaving Berne that Friday afternoon. They were jam-packed into the train and the air was full of "Ciao, Ciao," as they smiled and waved good-bye to friends. It turned out that I was returning to Italy with the Italian men working in Switzerland, who had a free trip home to vote. As usual, I had bought a third-class ticket that I might know more about the people and the country. There was no space anywhere, but I managed to squeeze into a first class compartment with five men, only one of whom had a ticket. First-class passengers were not travelling that day, as they evidently knew about the free trip for voters. Sam and Peg smiled and waved, delighted with the gaiety and good humour of everyone, but slightly apprehensive about the number jammed into the train. There was such a crowd the conductor never came to collect my ticket.

With five men talking to me or at me the whole time, I began to get tired. Trying to understand in another language can be fatiguing. The four men without tickets kept changing places to let men standing in the corridor have a chance to sit down. One man, who spoke a little English, proudly sang "God save the Queen" for me. Another told me, in great amazement, that he had once watched two Englishwomen talk for half and hour, and all they moved was their lips. The Italians enrich their conversations with so many gestures that I could understand his amazement.

I got off at Gallarate to catch my Varese train and, as my suitcase was handed down from the open window, I felt I was saying goodbye to real friends. The windows were packed with happy brown faces. All the men were eagerly holding out their money for drinks and food. The vendor went as fast as he could, but many went without as the train pulled away. I was impressed by the patient and good-humoured way they accepted this, just as I had been impressed by their acceptance of the crowded train trip.

Those of us waiting for our train seemed strangely drawn together. It was so peaceful, and as we waited there was the magic of an Italian spring night about us, even in under the roofs that protected the platforms. We talked quietly, and I had a feeling of great happiness as I was feeling so close to Italy and her people. I was even happier when, at a stop halfway to Varese, there was a gentle pressure on my arm; one of the women who had talked with me on the platform had come to shake my hand and bid me goodbye.

I had returned for the wedding of Bruna's eighteen year-old stepdaughter, Celestina, to her beloved Francesco. Bruna had told us that we were to be invited, and the young couple had delivered the invitation on their motor scooter. When you are invited to a wedding in Italy, you receive a small gift. Ours was the usual small china plate heaped with white sugar-coated almonds (known as *confetti* in Italy). The whole is tied up in white tulle and in among the almonds is a small piece of paper with the names of the bride and groom printed in silver. We consulted with Giannina as to the correct procedure. We were to have our gift in an attractive box and to take flowers.

When we arrived, a little before eleven in the morning, we were the only ones with flowers. Since our bouquet was more impressive than the bride's, Celestina carried ours. The bouquet she was going to carry was given to a delighted Maria Louisa, Bruna's daughter, who was wearing her new long white confirmation dress for the first time. There were strict instructions to try to keep it clean.

Kim and I, with a few relatives, were all gathered in the kitchen, having sweet cakes and wine. Everyone was having a turn at combing the curly hair of Ernesto, Celestina's brother. I wondered why such assiduous hair combing was necessary. We then discovered it was to be a double wedding. Ernesto was marrying his pretty Maria Assunta.

At eleven, Celestina came down the outside staircase from the bedrooms above. She was lovely, all in white. The sun shone, and her father and Bruna were waiting at the bottom of the stairs. We walked the few steps across the cobblestones to the church door, where the other bride and her family were waiting.

In Italy, no groom and his best man have to wait alone up at the altar. The groom walks up the aisle with his mother behind the bride and her father. The bride's mother and the groom's father walk up together and then take seats at the front. If you receive a formal printed invitation, the groom's name and family are on the right side, the bride's on the left, and across the bottom is the name and address of the church.

I could not follow much of the ceremony but enjoyed looking at the faces of the guests. Bruna was beaming. She was wearing her navy blue-serge suit and a white hat. The important thing at an Italian wedding (in the country at least) is to give the guests the best meal possible. A new outfit for the bride's mother is not even thought of.

When the ceremony in the church was over, a very touching one took place on the church steps. Maria Assunta's youngest sister, Luciana, then eleven and very smart in a tartan short dress, spread her arms in an expressive and appealing way, and made a touching speech wishing the two couples all happiness, and that their marriages be blessed with children.

There was a restaurant *cum* store across the road from the church. We all thronged into the two large rooms where, at other times, the men drank wine and played cards. It was shortly after twelve, and small iced cakes and champagne were served. During this time, the two brides and grooms slipped away to the cemetery that Celestina and her brother might have a few minutes with their mother, who is buried there. All the wedding flowers were left at her grave. When they returned, all of the wedding guests – there were sixty of us – walked along the road to visit Celestina and Francesco's apartment. It was in an old building and had a downstairs room that served as kitchen, dining room and living room. We took turns going in to look. Their bedroom was upstairs, but you had to come outside and then take a few steps to a loggia, walled on three sides but open on the one side. In here, a stairway led up to their bedroom. The Italians spend quite lavishly on their bedroom furniture, which is large and usually ornate. The double bed, known as a *matrimoniale*, is very wide, and when I thought of tiny Celestina washing those huge sheets by hand, I wondered how she would manage.

Suddenly, amidst much laughter, we were all shut out of the bedroom while the bride and groom were photographed in their bed. I could not find out what it was all about, but later they appeared flushed and smiling shyly and there was much more laughter and intimate joking.

Then we all walked up the hillside to see the other apartment, which was in a brand new building, very modern and all on the same floor. It consisted of a bright kitchen, with all modern conveniences; this was also the dining room-living room. The bedroom was large, with enormous furniture, and then a tiny bathroom. Since the other apartment was in an old building, they would wash in the kitchen and have a toilet at the back.

By now it was almost 2:00, and we walked back down the hillside to the restaurant. We started to eat at 2:00 and finally left the tables about 7:30. We were not eating all the time, and usually, between courses, wandered outside. The same dishes had to be used for the many courses and had to be quickly washed.

I marveled at the food supplied by those country people of limited means. We started with assorted cold meats and hors d'oeuvres. Then came three different courses of meat: chicken, beef and veal; and meat is very expensive in Italy. We had vegetables and salads and much wine. There was a contagious gaiety that no one could resist. There was singing and, as spirits rose, the sugar-coated almonds started to be thrown. I watched a shy, reserved farmer gradually lose his inhibitions and start throwing almonds. Years dropped away, and his eyes became the eyes of a daring, mischievous boy as he took aim and threw his almond. It could be quite painful if someone hit you fair and square, but it was all part of the fun.

Late in the afternoon, amidst all the happy noise, I heard someone mooing like a cow. It was a signal to Bruna that it was milking time. Bruna left us and walked down the road to her place. Her cows were devoted to her and allowed no one else to milk them. While we awaited her return, people wandered out on the balcony, admired each other's children and talked and talked and talked. Over the balcony railing, I made the acquaintance of Luigia Miraculo. She kept an old umbrella in her garden as a shelter for her one turkey. She had a smile like a sunburst. From then on, I always had a warm greeting any time I passed her place on my way down the road to Signor Bruno's boathouse apartment.

When Bruna returned, we went back to the tables for fruit, wedding cake and champagne. Almonds flew thick and fast. Some people lingered around the table, others visited on the balcony. We joined those dancing to records. The woman who had sat next to me at the table, a family cousin from the other side of Varese, was older and rather reserved. It was her husband that I watched change into an eager young boy. They had no children, a real tragedy for Italians who love children so dearly. When she found we had none either, it was a bond between us. She immediately took me under her wing; all barriers were down. There was such warmth and sincerity in her goodbyes that no one seeing us would ever have believed that we had only met at 2:00 that day. Everyone said their goodbyes at 11:30 that night.

Kim and I had fallen so completely under Italy's spell that we just had to share the beauty with others. Seventeen-year-old Duff, my sister Lib's younger son, had been making movies ever since he could hold a camera, and we thought anyone interested in movies should visit Italy. He arrived in June when his high school year ended.

Duff had been fortunate enough to have three seats to himself on the plane, and that night's sleep, fitful though it may have been, helped him through his first evening with us. After a long flight, one should have at least a day of complete rest. But for the first time there was a big dance at Ispra, and we whisked him off to it. We had Adrianna as a partner for him. She was a charming Italian girl, brought up in Egypt, who spoke English with a delightful accent. I will always treasure hearing her sing "Hang down your head, Tom Dooley," which became "Heng dawn your head, Tom Dooley." Through Adrianna, Duff had an entrée into the life of young Italians. Unfortunately, he was off on a bus trip with her and her group when the impressive fishing boat ceremony took place on our lake. June 29 is the festival of St. Peter and St. Paul. Because Peter was a fisherman, that is the day the priest in our church in Calcinate blessed the fishing boats. We tried to find out when the ceremony would begin and where. It seemed impossible to get definite information on such things. You are either expected to know or be clever enough to find out. We certainly tried to find out with no success, so started off for the church in the early evening. Halfway there, we met a big truck with the fine statue of the Infant Jesus being held upright by the choir in red cassocks and white surplices. The truck jogged in over the rough ground next to the grand, lakeside villa, where Maria was housekeeper. Three large boats were at the wharf. The swaying statue was carefully placed in the first boat with the priest, and the choir boarded the other boats. There were lighted candles all around the gunnels of the boats that cast a lovely light on the water. Quietly and with the grace of a ballet, the thirty-two fishermen rowed up from Calcinate.

Then the beautiful ceremony began. The priest's voice rang out, and the boats dipped and bobbed gracefully as they rowed out into the lake. They came right down past our villa. By then we had joined Mother on our balcony. How she gloried in the fine voice of the priest. They made a big sweep out into the lake, and, with all the twinkling candles, the voice of the priest, and the singing of the choir, it was pure beauty. Then came a jarring note. Fireworks were set off. The Italians seem to love noise; there were no fireworks bursting in the air, just terrific bangs.

The lovely singing was still floating across the water, but we could hardly hear it for the noise of the thunder crackers.

Next day, Signora Bottini told me that only at Easter and on the feast of St. Peter and St. Paul was the dome of St. Peter's in Rome illuminated. I wondered why these saints were so honoured, and then I realized that St. Peter is the patron saint of the cathedral. I had never heard of the *Sanpietrini*. They were the men who lit and placed the flares that illuminated the dome. For generations, these men, who were hereditary acrobats, trained their sons to be utterly fearless of heights. In olden times, many of them had abodes up on the roof of St. Peter's. These *Sanpietrini* also dug the tombs of the Popes. The more I learned about St. Peter's and the Vatican, the more impressed I was with the fascinating and complex organization responsible for the operation. On the first note of 9:00 p.m., the chief of the *Sanpietrini* lit the flare at the top of the cross on the dome of the cathedral. When the last note of 9:00 p.m. sounded, the 360 men had the whole dome illuminated.

While Duff missed seeing our fishing boats blessed, there was not much else that he missed. We celebrated his birthday with a trip to Isola Bella and Isola Pescatore. I made a joint birthday cake for Kim and Duff that I iced beautifully and, as I mentioned, I inadvertently stepped into it. Being ankle-deep in cake and icing is quite a sensation.

From the time he arrived, Duff just naturally went over the railing and down the tree that grew up through our balcony rather than use the steps. Whether it was descending that tree, or the old moviemaker at work, I never knew, but soon he was planning to film "Tarzan on the Lake of Varese."

Angelo had many swims and suppers with us, because Rina and the boys, like so many Italians, were away in the mountains for the month. I knew Angelo was to take two parts in the movie and Kim was to be the villain, but I saw no other Jane we could call on except myself. One day, I said, "Duff, I am too old to be Jane." I need not have worried. There was to be no Jane. I was to be Tarzan's mother who came to the aid of her strong, but not too bright, son.

I made a wig for Tarzan. It was so weird that, when a German friend tried it on, her dog turned on her with quite a fierce growl. Duff planned the movie very cleverly. While there was much work for him in the editing and splicing of the film, it was great fun for the rest of us. Kim and I, who had never used a movie camera, became fairly proficient.

According to Orson Welles, all Italians are actors, and the poorer ones are on the stage. I could believe it as the film progressed. Duff explained to Signor Bruno, who was to play the chief of police, what he wanted, and, with no rehearsal, Signor Bruno gave such a finished performance that no retake was necessary.

Angelo was both chauffeur and a prison guard, and wore his Alpine regimental uniform which, after all the years since the war, still fitted him perfectly. He was filmed at the Bottini's iron gates, and the sight of Angelo so trim and smart in a uniform from the last war brought many passing cars to a surprised halt. Angelo paused to reassure one lady driver, "No, Signora, I am not mad. We are making a film."

A white purse clutched in my teeth, in a sarong and swim fins, I had to go over the iron railing, down the tree and leap into the lake. With my newly learned jerky version of the crawl, I thrashed my way to Tarzan's rescue.

Giovanni was a worker in the prison and had to carry laundry out to the waiting laundry van driven by Angelo. Our villain, Kim, was to make his escape in a laundry bag. As Giovanni heaved the laundry bag over his shoulder, he managed to entangle a very feminine slip that the Bottini's maid, Maria, had drying over a bush. Giovanni's nonchalant removal of that slip was so perfect that Duff left it in the film.

While Duff planned, organized and worked hard, we had great fun and learned many tricks of the trade.

Then we had yet another dance. The summer before there had been no organized social life, but now the French had a dance in honour of the freeing of the Bastille. It was held in the European School, where children of the Euratom staff received their education. This school is a fine, well-designed building in which children can be educated in French, German, or Italian. Kim and I made the most of our chance to explore it. The dance was a lively one. Many of the French came in their regional costumes and brought cakes of their region. French exuberance can be a bit wild at times. Fireworks were set off right on the dance floor, something I could have done without. I like rockets to go up, not swish about my ankles.

When there was a full moon to make our lake even more beautiful, we gave a party ourselves. There were twelve of us for dinner and dancing, and without Duff's help I don't think I could have thought of it. Preparing dinner for twelve in that minute kitchen took real organization, but we managed it.

What we call Japanese lanterns, the Italians call Venetian lanterns. There was no wind or breeze, so the candlelight shone softly in the lanterns hung in the trees and on the balcony. The four male guests arrived with their arms full of lovely flowers, adding yet more beauty to the evening. I have always been delighted to receive flowers, but especially so in Italy.

It was a perfect evening and a perfect party. Duff and I danced the Charleston. In Ugo Bottini's pronunciation, it came out as the "Charlie Stone," and we had orders for lessons. This time Duff's partner for the evening was the German girl, Carola, who spoke perfect English and whose dog had growled at her in Tarzan's wig.

Duff was able to tour Rome with one of Catherine's sons, who also spoke English. Kim had to go on business, so Duff went along and stayed with Catherine and her four children. He had a chance to see home life and many of the sights of Rome.

One evening, Varese put on a *son et lumiere* spectacle in the lovely gardens of the old palace opposite the Albergo Europa. It was a history of Tyrolean music, and was a masterpiece of showmanship. The singing was beautiful and the dancing gay and lively. Suddenly, one part of the garden would be floodlit and a man in colourful Tyrolean costume would be cutting wood and singing. Then another part would be lit and a maid and a man would be on the hillside singing. The glorious, floodlit old trees were an entertainment in themselves, but the lovely music and dancing made an unforgettable evening. A pleasant surprise for us was that one of the handsome young waiters from the hotel was one of the dancers. His coming up in costume and speaking so charmingly to us fairly melted Mother's heart.

The weekend we took Duff to Merano was a holiday, and also Bimbi's birthday, so we had Bimbi and Reinier to show us special places up on the mountain tops. We took a lift up, and for two days we walked up there. The mountain flowers, the air, the rustic beauty of the farm buildings, were all you could ask for. We lunched on rough wooden tables out under trees. For the first time, Duff had *kaiserschmarm*, an Austrian type of thin pancake served with raisins and raspberry syrup. We found this so delicious we went back the second day for lunch. Duff said that the girl he married would have to know how to make *kaiserschmarm*.

That evening down in Merano, we had dinner out-of-doors again, this time in an old courtyard, and for the first time in Europe listening to zither music.

Madame Burg invited us for tea the next day. The main hall was a bit disordered, for she had been robbed of her collection of fabulous old guns belonging to the Hapsburg family. Fortunately, the police had recovered the guns but they had not yet been put back in the big glass case.

"Would Duff be interested in guns and would he like to examine them?" Guns were a passion with Duff at that time. He more than examined them; he practically fondled them. I will never forget his face as he bent over those guns. "I have seen them in museums, but to be able to touch them..."

On our way home, we stopped in Verona and were lucky enough to get tickets for the opera "Aida." This opera, performed in the Coliseum, was a spectacle to end all spectacles. There was a full moon, an orchestra of 100, and sometimes 500 actors were pouring onto the stage. The scenery and costumes were lavish and Aida and her father had very fine voices. With the great full moon overhead, the whole evening had a dream-like quality. As they filed into the Coliseum, many of the audience had been given candles. With the first notes of music, like magic, the candles were lit and for the time that they burned, the candlelight twinkling like stars in that old stone Coliseum was so lovely that my Italian tears flowed.

Duff took a trip on his own into Switzerland and had a visit with our Swiss friends and their three children. He was very much on my mind until he returned, and I gave a great sigh of relief when I heard his Tarzan yell as he came down the lane past the barn. We hated to have him leave us, but he was meeting his mother in England to have a great time in England and Scotland.

One memory he and I will always share. We were standing on the balcony looking down into the lake and saw two fish mating. It was like a ballet. Every movement was fluid grace.

Duff's mother, Elizabeth, is my younger sister. There is a difference of only two years in our ages, and, when we were small, we were known as "the heavenly twins." Oddly enough, this was because we could be so full of mischief. We had shared a great deal over the years, and I was keen to have her get to know Italy, for I knew what would appeal to her.

Elizabeth, or Lib, was to come on to Italy after the jaunt with her son in England and Scotland. Her letter said she would arrive in Milan at five in the morning. We were there to meet her, but she was not on the train. We returned to Varese dejected, and spent the day awaiting developments. Apparently she arrived on another train at a different station and, through a series of brave initiatives, helped by an Italian who spoke some English, she managed to get to Varese, engage a taxi and give him our address at the lake.

No sight was ever more welcome to me than seeing that taxi coming around the corner of the barn. I was so worried all day that I did not know what to do, and was trying to do a little gardening. I simply flew to her. The driver was left in no doubt as to our happiness in being together.

The next day was a Saturday, and Kim drove us down to Milan to pick up Lib's luggage and show her some of the sights. Having just come from London, she was interested to learn that London's banking street, Lombard Street, got its name from the banks of Lombardy, this province, that was instrumental in setting up the English banking system. Also that pounds, shillings and pence got their symbols from the ancient Roman system of *librum*, *solidus* and *dinarius*.

Lib loved our house and its location. If I was outside and called to her, she would pop out an open door and say,"Reporting on balcony number one."

Tina and Alessandro, her son, had not yet returned to Spain, and it was most interesting for Lib to talk to Tina and to get a young Italian's point of view. Italians were such realists about many things. They never seemed to have any illusions. I often wondered if in our part of the world advertising has so coloured or clouded our reasoning that it gives us a fairy tale outlook. Many Italian women I met took it as a matter of course that their husbands would be unfaithful to them. They had a lover until their first child was born. Then he became a father, and it was human nature for him to stray. I did tell Libby that while they were such realists, they had no way to contend with partings; all was grief and tears then.

This was what I wanted for Lib's visit. Not only was Tina a great help in letting Lib know how an Italian woman felt, she also drove us to beautiful villas and introduced us to friends she felt we would find interesting.

Lib had hardly arrived before she was off on her travels again. Kim had his heart set on a new car, a Peugeot, and had to go up to France to pick it up. We had no trouble selling our Fiat, even though it had had a winter ducking. When they got back, Kim just had time to show me the new gearshift, then was off to report to Canada.

Mother agreed to go to Lugano for a stay in a hotel, so I could take Lib on a brief tour of Italy. Tina drove us to Lugano in our new car, as my managing of the new gearshift left something to be desired. We installed Mother in a comfortable hotel and I prayed for English-speaking companions for her.

We left on our tour the next morning, me with my dictionary close at hand. Going from Milan to Genoa, Lib had her first *chestini* lunch on the train. I left Lib sitting with our luggage in the Genoa station while I walked to the nearest hotel. In my best Italian, I said I was a Canadian and did not speak Italian well. I got no further, for they graciously said "O, *la Signora parla bene, bene.*" All relaxed, I made the arrangements for our room. Once we were settled in, we made our way to see Pina Beltrami, who once had rented her apartment to Kim's aunt. Lib heard her unlock her seven locks on the door to the apartment. The people of Genoa feel that, since it is a port city, they must be especially careful to protect themselves. I have never seen nor imagined such a complicated system of locks.

It was raining hard in Genoa, but, rain or no rain, Pina was determined Lib should see Genoa, so we were off on a whirlwind tour. We saw a beautiful villa that changed hands during a game of cards. We visited the ancient university. We could feel its atmosphere and were moved by its impressive staircase. To save time and to give us a bit of respite from the drenching rain, Pina would whip us into a great church and trot us across it, which was like cutting across a city block. I had already found that churches in Italy were not dim and silent to be used only on Sundays. They were a part of the people's lives, a place to drop in any time for a prayer and a gossip. Once, in a remote country church, during a Palm Sunday service, Kim and I heard a dog fight right in the church. The priest just waited until the snarling died down enough for him to be heard. Neither Lib nor I were at all comfortable about using churches as a short cut, but Pina took it as a matter of course.

Rome was to be our next stop. The train to Rome obligingly slowed down and gave us a fine view of the famous Leaning Tower of Pisa. Many of the stations along the way were pocked with bullet holes, showing us where the war had passed. As we neared Rome, we were intrigued to see that, where the arches of the old Roman aqueduct were low enough, human dwellings had been achieved by closing in the front and back of the arch.

In the station at Rome, I had trouble using the telephone and went for help to a group of smart and flashy young women who were sitting at tables. At first they were quite hostile, but then one came to my rescue. Later, I found out they were prostitutes.

Once I got Catherine on the phone, she told me of a reasonable and central hotel.

The Church of Santa Maria Maggiore was across the square from our hotel, so that was our first call next morning. We heard that the gold plating on the ceiling was given by Queen Isabella of Spain, gold that had been a gift to her from Christopher Columbus. I had always wondered why Italy did not support his search. It was maintained, at the time, that if he was successful in finding an alternate route to the Orient, Italy would lose its monopoly as a centre of trade with the Orient by the overland route. The Spaniards on the other hand had everything to gain.

Next, we walked over and saw the Coliseum in the blazing sun, and wondered how the Romans could have endured the glare. We learned there used to be a huge awning manipulated by sailors from the Adriatic. It could not be used on windy days. We also learned that, if the gladiators had fought exceptionally well, some were allowed to appeal for life. If the audience, sometimes as many as eighty thousand, gave the "thumbs up" sign, *mite* (let him go), it was the tradition that the man was spared. "Thumbs down" *jugula* meant "kill him."

We took a few guided tours, and sometimes the people we saw gave us almost as much entertainment as the things we saw. We were in a very handsome church that had as its relic the chains that had bound St. Paul. There was a harassed, middle-aged woman on the tour, clutching not one but two overstuffed black purses. Libby and I were looking at a really magnificent statue of Moses when she dashed up breathless and frantic: "The chains, the chains, where are the chains?" she cried. Now we have only to whisper to each other "the chains, the chains" and we are off in giggles.

The traffic in Rome lived up to its reputation: chaotic. It gave us one of the best laughs of our lives. It was late afternoon, and traffic was heavy and definitely out of hand. In the middle of the snarl was the policeman, slim and elegant in his spotless white uniform. Up on his podium, he was waving his baton with all the grace of a man conducting a symphony. Things were going from bad to worse. Suddenly, to our amazement and delight, he threw up his arms in despair, jumped down and left them to work out the mess for themselves.

We saved our visit to St. Peter's to the last. We went early in the morning, and saw many black figures hurrying across the piazza carrying small black suitcases. We found out they were priests. It is a privilege to say mass in St. Peter's. The priests book months in advance. We realized mass after mass was being said at various altars.

Lib saw where the toes of the statue of St. Peter had been worn away by devout kisses. We ended our tour with Michelangelo's "Pieta," wondering how, in stone, he could express such tragedy and feeling, and how anything as hard as marble could seem to tremble.

Lib and I wondered why some statues in the Vatican had fig leaves. I found out that this was due to a pope, Hadrian or Adrian, a man of very strict views who got very little sympathy from the Italians. He had been shocked by the nude statues and had ordered fig leaves put over the offending parts. The Italians found this hard to take. When Hadrian died, in about 750 A.D., their delightful Italian sense of humour prompted them to hang a wreath of honour on the door of his physician.

Rome had cast its spell on us, but we had to move on to Florence. In the railway station at Florence we were delighted to find a directory of hotels and pensions, and a very competent man to phone and make our reservations. We decided to be thrifty and try a pension. We were not at all impressed with the bathroom, but made do. The highlight of our visit was a *carozza* ride. It was late afternoon, and I asked the driver sitting in his carriage what the fare would be. He said he would take us for a half-hour ride for 1,000 lira. He did not seem friendly.

One and a half hours later, his horse was still clop-clopping along, and Libby and I were straining to see all that our driver pointed out. Whether it was my Italian or our interest in every-thing, or a combination of both, he could not have been more friendly. We saw where Michelangelo had rested, famous build-ings, the statue of David, all the glory of Florence. He told us that, in a church we were passing, children had been confirmed earlier in the day and now were making their first communion. Would we like to slip in and look? He and his horse waited pa-tiently while we stood inside the door and felt the peace and solemnity of the service.

Our driver's courtesy had given a glow to the whole evening. We walked the streets until bedtime.

Our next day in Florence, I made sure Lib got to see all the buildings she had seen from the outside. The paintings left her as overwhelmed as they had overwhelmed me. Once more I could not find the memorial tablet to Florence Nightingale, who was born in this city and is reputed to be the first woman to have the name "Florence."

The station in Venice had the same directory service we had found in Florence, and a pleasant clerk booked us a room in a small hotel. A launch took us to the stop for our hotel and a porter was waiting to show us the way and carry our bags.

After dinner we set out to explore. There had been a storm, and high winds had brought water washing in around the Cathedral and Saint Mark's square. The arrangement of planks to walk on was so good, we decided it must be needed often. The square was rather deserted, but, as is the custom, the orchestras of the restaurants played in turn. The musicians were all seated up on trestles to avoid the water. Two young men were so impressed with Venice and with the beauty of the night that they treated us to an impromptu ballet. They danced through the water in the Piazza as though it was not there.

Brilliant sunshine the next day prompted us to take a motor cruise of the islands. Murano was our first stop. The glass-blowing industry was moved from Venice to Murano in the thirteenth century to avoid the danger of fire to the ever more crowded city. In those days the export of Venetian glass was second only to the sea borne commerce. We watched skilled craftsmen blow through pipes to which the molten glass was attached. The soft blobs of glass would take on amazing shapes and then be cut off with scissors. I asked where the sand for the glass came from and was surprised when they told me Versailles, France.

Burano, the fishing centre famous for its lace, was our next stop. Here we watched old ladies and very young girls working on the intricate designs, and noted that hardly any were wearing glasses. A stiff breeze was blowing, and everyone had a washing flapping. The lines were brought down from the pole to the ground and smaller articles fitted on the slanted lines, handkerchiefs coming last. In a painting of Canaletto's, I was delighted to see that they hung their washing this way in his day.

Our launch moored next at the end of a lagoon. We could easily have walked to Torcello, but decided to treat ourselves to our first ride in a gondola. The gondola rides in Venice are expensive, but understandably so when you know of the maintenance and the cleaning that must be done to these boats. The silver-plated fittings and ornaments of little sea horses are usually passed on from father to son, as gondoliering runs in families.

Our gondolier, like so many, rowed cross-armed. He was dark-skinned and had black hair. His eyes were blue as sapphires. There are many fair-haired, blue-eyed Venetians.While our gondolier did not sing to us, he could not have been more charming.

Next day, the skies opened and it poured rain. We found much to see indoors. We spent the morning at the cathedral and the afternoon in the fabulous Doges' Palace. I knew Lib would be impressed with the great council chamber and Tintoretto's "Paradiso" with the faces of five hundred noblemen. They say you should either begin or end your visit to Venice by climbing up the bell tower of the Cathedral and looking out over the city. In the late afternoon the rain obligingly ended, and we made the climb.

We were so delighted with Venice that it came as quite a shock to us to have a young Venetian say there was no way he could stay on. He had no future in Venice. He said he could only be a shopkeeper, work in the hotel business or try to be a gondolier.

Verona was our next city to visit. Sad to say, we arrived at noon so the Coliseum was closed for the siesta period. We walked around it and, as by now I knew Verona well enough to be quite a competent guide, I gave Lib a good tour.

We were going on to Merano. I bought our tickets for Bolzano, as we had to change there for Merano. The trip up in the train was especially thrilling for me, as I was seeing parts I had never seen from the car.

In Bolzano, I left Lib at a table on the station platform. She said,"Don't order for me. I am sure I can do it now." I met my Waterloo at the ticket office. The clerk may have been one of the rebellious types who insisted on speaking German, but for the first time I met a stone wall: no way would he understand me. I was determined to get Lib to Merano in the daylight. After all, it was my card of the castles in Merano that had brought her over to Italy. I found a taxi driver who understood my Italian and went back for Libby. I found her sheepishly drinking hot chocolate. She had told me she was going to order orangeade, so something had gone wrong.

I knew Lib would love Merano, and she did. It was the time of the grape harvest and the district was awash with fresh grape juice. Bimbi's mother took us on a walking tour along the mountainsides where, at various places, you stopped to drink the juice. She cautioned us not to drink much because "one's bowels are not accustomed to it." Merano is famous for the "grape cure," where one subsists on the juice for two or three days. The result is to be completely cleaned out. The juice was delicious, but we heeded her warning and contented ourselves with the sunshine and the scenery.

We spent time watching the little channels and waterways that let people have water from the mountainside for their gardens. Suddenly there would be a gush of water, the channel would fill, then the flow would cease and the next garden would have its turn.

On the train back to Milan we realized, from the tension among the people and their scrutiny of newspapers, that something awful had happened. I finally managed to see a headline and looked up the word *diga*, meaning "dam." We later learned that there had been a tragedy at a hydro dam at Vaiont, in the north-eastern province of Friuli. Half a mountain had sideslipped into the reservoir above the dam. The dam had held, but a great wave had poured over the dam and had wiped out a sleeping village at its foot.

The only time we had to hurry on our whole trip was in Milan, where we had to cut short our good meal in the station restaurant and make a dash for the Varese train.

The next day, Tina drove us over to Lugano to pick up Mother. Once more, she had found almost no one to speak English with. She was delighted to get back to her own quarters, even if she had to shout *"Via, via"* at intruders.

The day after that, Kim was back from Canada and we had news and pictures of family. Signor Bruno, smartly dressed as usual, came to see if we wished to renew our lease. After the septic tank that had faltered and given up, and our pipes that had frozen, he seemed surprised at how happily we signed the lease for another year.

Observe that Kate, with experience of only a year in Italy and with still faltering Italian, took her sister on a tour encompassing Genoa, Rome, Florence, Verona, Bolzano and Merano, and back to Milan and Varese, making all the travel arrangements in Italian, acting as a guide and interpreter, as well as being a special companion. She was justly proud of her accomplishment, as indeed I was.

Chapter 11

Our Last Months in Italy

The Vaninis, from whom we rented our octagonal pagoda home, were the owners of one of the *patisseries* in Lugano, offering superb chocolates and delicious cakes. We often treated ourselves to their delicacies and to tea that was served in glasses fitted into metal frames with handles. They invited the four of us, Kim and me and Mother and Lib, together with Signor Bruno, their agent, for dinner one evening. We drove over in Signor Bruno's car. Their home, like many of the wealthy in Lugano, was built down the steep side of a mountain, one side being mountain and the other all windows looking out over the Lake of Lugano. The house had its own elevator, and we went down with it to an elegant drawing room. Our meal was absolute perfection. The tablecloth was so beautiful that it brought a gasp of admiration from me. It was organdy with lovely flowers appliquéd on it. My admiring it out loud was not a social mistake, for our host had given it to his wife for an anniversary gift. There were many fine paintings, and when our hostess saw I was interested, she took me down a few more floors and showed me yet more paintings.

I was so pleased this invitation came when Lib could be included. When you are traveling, you seldom get a chance to see private homes, and how the other half lives. Here, they certainly lived well.

It was while Lib was with us that Gianfranco, received the notice of his military training. Lib had seen on the sides of many homes a large chalked "Classe" with a number after it. This lets others know the date of the occupant's military training. If a passerby happens to be the same year, a great reunion can take place. A widow's eldest son is exempt from service, but all other young men, when they reach eighteen, must take training for eighteen months. Gianfranco, smiling shyly, came down with a box for contributions. All those in the district who had received their notice were collecting. The amount collected determines the extent of the celebration. They always buy jaunty hats and scarves and go on a happy outing to some nearby place. In the evening, they have a feast and sometimes a dance. The military service is mixing the population. On holidays, or when training is over, a chap brings home a new friend from a different part of Italy, who sometimes falls in love with a sister. After the marriage, the two families visit back and forth and then the grandchildren have holidays with their other grandparents.

Alessandro Bogni (of the family that was so helpful when our car took its plunge) brought home his new friend from San Remo, who lost his heart to lovely Luciana. The wedding took place while Lib was still with us and while she was not invited, we could tell her all about it.

The Bogni family was doing very well with their plastic business. Their home was on a rise of land and had a fine view of the lake and the mountains. The factory is on the ground level, and their smart, modern home is on the second floor. We were invited to the reception only. It and two others were being held in a large restaurant out in the country. The party down in the basement had really gotten underway when we arrived, judging from the singing and laughter. Upstairs we were two very happy groups, one facing one side of the room and the second group, the other. The groom and his parents were in the flower-growing business in San Remo, and our tables were strewn with white carnations. There were no long speeches, just a few sentences. From downstairs would come great bursts of song and laughter. There was no throwing of almonds this time. The bride and groom walked around the tables talking with each person and spooning out of a silver box a few of the white candy-coated almonds.

Whenever clapping started, the newlyweds had to kiss. There was a great show of making sure they realized there were two baby dolls in the ornament on the cake. Once, when Luciana had placed her veil and flowers on the head table, an uncle quickly put the veil on his head and swept the bouquet to his heart. Quick as a wink, the men near him gathered up carnations and showered him with flowers.

I knew a number of the local women, and recognised their dresses as their best. Once more, there was no buying of new dresses.

In later years, our newlyweds did have two children. You are never in any doubt as to when a baby has arrived. An enormous blue or pink bow appears on the door. My butcher's daughter in Gavirate was expecting, and when her baby was born, the butcher shop sported a blue bow and there were congratulations and compliments. You never mistake a baby's gender when you look into a baby carriage. The bow lets you know. Babies are christened within two weeks, and all the ones in our neighbourhood were helped into the world by a midwife. The mother has no anaesthetic. It is considered not good for her or the baby. Country babies are wrapped in swaddling clothes or bound for the first month. Lib thoroughly approved of this, as she had always bound her babies at night when they were small. She felt they slept better and did not get uncovered.

We hated for Lib to leave, but I was glad we were still having good weather, for I knew only too well how it could rain. Her departure was as peaceful as her arrival had been hectic. We drove in leisurely fashion over to Lugano, and waited on the open-air station platform looking down to the blue, blue lake. We were able to help her right into her compartment and stow her luggage.

Shortly after Lib left, we received a telegram from Sueo, a Japanese scientist and friend from Deep River days. His "Meet me if you can, I have no Italish" had us waiting at the station for him. His government had given him money for things he might need, and he had treated himself to a movie camera. A Saturday trip to Lugano produced a real show for him. As we arrived, a special wedding party came along. First there was a coach and four white horses, with white crocheted caps for their head. I had never seen a horse in Italy that did not have his ears covered, and this was a special covering. Next came eight black horses and black carriages. The drivers were all in black and wore tall silk hats. In the rear came brown horses. This was the one and only time we saw such a procession. It was pure delight for all of us, especially for Sueo.

I knew from Deep River days that Sueo loved fruit. The persimmons had the nip of frost that makes them perfect, so that evening I served them for dessert. Imagine our surprise to discover their name in Italian and Japanese was the same, *Cacchi*. We learned there are over 700 Portugese words in the Japanese language dating from the early trade between the two countries.

Sueo was with us only three days, but his camera was very busy. When his thank you letter arrived, it said,"I will never forget my good time at there with you."

Sueo loved our outside staircase and took a number of snaps of it. I did not love that outside staircase quite so much for the next few weeks. Just as it did the year before, it started to rain on November first, and rained almost steadily most of November. Making trips down to my laundry tub, the downstairs sitz tub, was not easy in that steady downpour. Whenever the rain let up a bit, I would dash out with my umbrella and garbage and do my best to get a fire going. I had many a hysterical giggle crouched under that umbrella, and at other times I ground my teeth and muttered "sunny Italy," as my eyes smarted from the smoke. We were more than tired of the days and days of rain, but there was a silver lining. A crop of delicious mushrooms had sprung up along the banks of the stream. They thrived in the rain, and oh, how we enjoyed them.

We did have a lovely weekend to look back on. It was the last one in October and was a long holiday. We still had some of our holidays left, so we took Thursday off, as we wanted to go to Innsbruck to buy new skis. We had been a bit too trusting and had left ours outside down under where we kept the car. When we were away in the spring, someone had taken them. We knew it had to have been by night and by water. From our car immersion, we knew how well our place was watched by daylight, and we knew if anyone had used the lane by night, Fritz would have barked until Giovanni came.

We made it to our beloved hotel Bardolino for lunch. This was our fifth visit, and the manager, the two cooks and the three waitresses gave us a royal welcome. We started off with truffles and noodles. The truffles are found in the woods around Verona and are hunted out with dogs. We were hoping to stay in Merano, but Mother was so tired we made Bolzano our stop. We were lucky enough to get rooms in a charming old hotel right on the square. It is reputed to be one of the oldest hotels in Europe and it certainly had atmosphere and great peace. Kim and I spent the evening exploring the city in a gentle rain. It is a picturesque old place and has a beautiful old church, famous for its airy spire. It reminded us of St. Giles in Edinburgh.

Next morning we left Mother comfortably settled and took off for Innsbruck. The drive through the Brenner Pass I will never forget. The mountains were breathtaking in their grandeur. The larch trees had turned golden, and, in among the dark green evergreens, they were lovely. The tops of the mountains were white with snow, but the slopes were still green. Our lunch in a little Austrian inn was delicious. The doors of the inn were so attractive with all their gaily painted flowers and designs, I was tempted to tamper with the hinges and try for a get-away.

Innsbruck delighted us. It was spacious, friendly and had fascinating old buildings. The decorations and carved wood had us taking many pictures. We stayed overnight in a historic old inn, advertised as a favourite of Goethe's. A couple of friendly young men on the sidewalk outside the inn told us the beds were as hard as when Goethe had slept there. We did not find them so, but I did have to take out the huge wedge-shaped pillow.

Since the purpose of our trip was to replace our stolen skis, off we went bright and early the next morning. We were very satisfied with the ones we bought and the service we received. Kim's German was a big help.

We bought bread, wine, meat and cheese and had a picnic up where we could smell the evergreens and hear the running water. In all my time in Italy, I had only seen one slightly drunk Italian, and he was an old man selling lavender in a market. We were quite surprised at the number of young Austrians who had had just a bit too much. We had visited a tavern Friday evening so knew how pleasant they were. As we drove away from the city, two pleasant, slightly drunk young men waved us off.

We got back to Bolzano in time for dinner. It always came as a surprise to me how much you could see in such a short time in Europe. After Austria's sunshine, it was hard to come back to the rain. Mother was a good sport and agreed to stop over Sunday night at Bardolino. While the food was renowned, the rooms were like those you might find in an old farmhouse.

We arrived about 3:00, and after getting Mother settled for a siesta, we went exploring up the hillside through vineyards and olive groves. We tried the green olives off the tree, but had to spit them out as they were too bitter. We just got in from our walk when the rain came down in torrents. After yet another delicious dinner and an evening's repose, the rain let up enough to allow us a walk along the lakeshore. We had fallen in love with a stately old villa, famous for its roses. All we could find out about it was that it had been built for an artist, Christallo, from Verona. The wrought ironwork, its graceful staircase and the detail around the windows captivated Kim and me. We would stand, enchanted, looking in through the elaborate railings to the display of roses.

Monday was Victory Day and the church nearby woke us early with much bell ringing. It was an experience to look out our bedroom windows and see and hear only the local people, no tourists about. We left early to get home before the heavy weekend traffic got moving. Every town and village was having a Victory Parade. Some of the music was weird and wonderful, provided by an odd assortment of musicians and instruments. There were many veterans resplendent with medals and many marchers of all ages. This was peaceful, but the serious faces of the two soldiers we had seen guarding every bridge from Bolzano down to Lago di Garda reminded us that there were those who could make trouble.

We drove down our lane about 4:00 in the afternoon, to be greeted by a smiling Giovanni under one of his tattered umbrellas. He was checking to see how much the lake had risen. He and our *porta lettera* again checked it daily. It rose and rose and finally we had only three feet of lawn left. The little stream that ran down past the barn and our driveway had become a raging torrent. Mother had become quite apprehensive. Thank goodness she did not understand Italian, or she would have been really frightened. In the worst rain, this stream that runs under Giovanni's house rose so high it finally ran right through the house. The great disaster of that flood was that the gushing water carried Giannina's much-loved parrot down to the lake and his death. She had such a wonderful relationship with her chickens and turkeys, I could only imagine how close she and her parrot must have been.

Perhaps it was day after day of rain, or just that she had enough of being left out of Italian conversation, but Mother decided she was going back to the States before Christmas. The night we took her to the Albergo Europa for a goodbye dinner, the Stabilinis had us over to their table afterwards. They produced one of the last ten of a hundred bottles of wine they had bought in 1943. It was like a very light port and very fine. Mother appreciated the honour, but the conversation was mostly Italian as only two of the five Stablinis spoke any English. Mother was once more left out, but she whispered to me "my day is coming." She was twinkling in her excitement and anticipation. The goodbyes between her and the waiters were very moving.

The next day, a Sunday, we were invited to Italian friends for the midday meal. I got us up early and gave us a light breakfast so we would be able to cope with the large and delicious Piedmonte meal I knew we would have. Their young son, who spoke no English – neither did his mother – offered me a candy and confided to me seriously that if I ate it I would have to go to the dentist.

After three weeks of rain, we finally had sunshine again. It was the weekend of November 22 and we drove up into the Dolomites to try to find a place to ski and spend Christmas. We had found the previous Christmas so sad and lonely, and since Mother would be gone, too, we knew it would be hard to spend Christmas by ourselves, so we decided to keep ourselves busy on the ski slopes.

It was too late to find anything through an agency, so we set off to see what we could find. We checked into the hotel in Bolzano that Mother had found comfortable three weeks before. Our pleasure that weekend was clouded by news of President Kennedy's death.

You always had to hand in your passport at the hotel desk on checking in. Mother's passport was so precious to her that she was always reluctant to part with it. She could not see why they had to have it again, when they had studied it such a short time before. Kim and I had been at the cinema in the afternoon to see a Hitchcock film *"The Birds"* that had left us in quite an upset state. When we came into the hotel, the man on the desk handed us back the passports. He put his hand on Mother's U.S. passport and said in Italian,"He is dead." All I caught was "is dead." I thought for a moment that Mother had died, so it was a double shock for me. He was speaking of President Kennedy. We sat up for hours listening to my little transistor radio. Neither of us slept much that night. The Italians are warm-hearted. They loved Kennedy and held him in high esteem. Their reaction was one of great grief. The American Army stations were over-whelmed by the condolences. All flags were produced and flown at half-mast, cinemas were closed and churches held special masses. A young boy of twelve, in Bergamo, who had idolized Kennedy, took a treasured photograph and a bunch of red roses, and went into a quiet park and shot himself. There was grief and sadness everywhere.

We were a very thoughtful couple as we drove up one of the valleys in the Dolomites. When we found the spot we felt would have the most sunshine and decided that it looked to have the best ski slopes, we had the incredible good luck to get the last double room with bath in the hotel. We liked the look of the proprietress and felt we would have good food.

We ate our lunch in a small mountain inn and when news of Kennedy came on the radio, men who were eating left their tables and crowded around the radio. The only times I had seen Italian men leave their food was for an important soccer game. When they returned to their tables, one man said to us,"He was a good man. He was working for the world."

We saw Mother off for New York on December 4, and the house seemed empty and still without her. I missed her greatly. If the *porta lettera* had no mail for us and I did not go shopping, some days I would speak to no one until Kim came home at night. I was fortunate to have Signora Bottini up the hillside, Giannina and Giovanni and our friends in Calcinate and Gropello. The weather was crisp and cold now and, with dictionary in hand, I went visiting, and my Italian improved.

Kim had a conference at the University of Bologna, December 17, 18 and 19, so with all our ski equipment in the car, we set off. There seemed to be a jinx on Kim's clothes and Bologna. He drove in knickers and knee socks, and though he had packed a good supply of ski socks, we discovered he had not packed any ordinary socks. Bologna was deep in snow, with great icicles hanging on the famous Neptune statue in a frozen fountain. As soon as the shops opened in the morning, Kim and I were waiting to buy socks. I was along to take the extra pairs back to the hotel. I was remembering our first trip when Bruno had engaged Kim in such violent conversation that he had forgotten to pack underwear, and with my scant Italian and no knowledge of men's sizes in Italy, I had shopped for him. I would have loved a picture of the surprised face of the salesman as Kim took off his shoes and put the socks on his bare feet. The man looked out into the snowy streets and you could see him thinking, "He walked here with no socks on."

I myself had a surprise that day, and it was a lovely one. As I was walking the streets I heard odd, lamenting music and came upon a pair of shepherds in the unusual garb they wear as they play their Christmas tribute to the Virgin.

On the twentieth, we set off on our drive to Plan di Gralba, in the Dolomites. There was snow and the roads were icy. After years of Canadian winter driving, Kim took it all in his stride. Not so the Italian drivers. They were just creeping along. It was the first time I had seen slow and cautious driving in Italy.

Kim had to keep his eyes on the road, but mine were taking in every detail of the barns of old silvered wood. Some were of logs and blended into the landscape as though they had grown and not been built. I realized the streams would be raging torrents in the spring, for many of the huge rocks were as smooth and round as old cannon balls. As we drove north, we kept wondering if we would have enough snow. We knew that Madonna di Campiglio was short of it.

Christmas spirit was running high with us, and as we passed cemeteries, the little votive candles twinkling away in the walls seemed like Christmas lights. One shrine up on a hillside, all shining with candles, looked almost like a Christmas tree.

We need not have worried about snow, for it lay deep up in the Dolomites. We need not have worried about Christmas spirit either. An American family stationed in Milan were in our hotel for their second Christmas. There were three boys: George was just old enough to ski, Jerry was old enough to sleigh ride and the baby old enough to gurgle in a high chair.

These three plus the granddaughter of the proprietress – a sunbeam of a child – and a quiet, dark German girl holidaying with her mother, generated enough Christmas spirit for the whole hotel. We had a fine big Christmas tree, which had to be taken down the day after Christmas, as the hotel kitten thought it had been placed there for him to climb, and the pretty butter sugar cookies tied all over it had been placed there for him to crunch.

The tree was thrown down outside, close to a little stream. This stream made it quite a long jaunt to get to a ski tow. What I needed was a bridge over that stream, so I set to work with that big, bushy tree. I was patting snow and bits of wood into my bridge and looked up to see one of the Italian guests watching me intently. He, his wife and two daughters had been very friendly. His close scrutiny of my work had me wanting to say, "And what do you know about bridge building?" I was so glad my Italian did not go that far, for it turned out that he was one of Italy's foremost builders of bridges. He was Pier Emilio Braussi, city engineer for Ancona, and in charge of the work of repairs to war damage. As the days passed, we became firm friends with the family, and have remained friends to this day.

My bridge turned out so well that before long many skiers were taking my shortcut. The skiing and the sunshine were all you could ask for. We often had the hotel make up a lunch for us because all the tows stopped at noon, for the workers to have their meals. The middle of the day was a grand time to be up on the higher slopes, just basking in the sunshine. As we opened our lunches, I always chuckled over the six toothpicks.

Speaking of chuckling, everyone always knew when Joe was going to fall. Joe was a Siamese student holidaying with German university friends. In the hotel he charmed us all with his sunny disposition and his determination to master the art of skiing. Always just before he fell, his marvelous, oriental giggle would be heard, and we all chuckled with him.

We also had a good laugh provided by a new guest who was not accustomed to the thin walls of ski chalets. We heard in a very agitated Italian, "Who is it, who is it?" There was no answer, and then, in an even more high-pitched agitated voice, we again heard, "Who is it, who is it?" Then we heard, "What do you mean 'who is it?' I'm in my own bathroom."

There was everything to make it a happy holiday. The food was good, though more Austrian than Italian. We had a real turkey dinner Christmas Day, and every woman received a gift. Mine was a dainty little Capo de Monte candlestick.

It was interesting to observe the different food tastes. The Americans came with cranberry sauce, which I longed to share. Two German couples, who ate at the table next to ours, always brought down cold meats, sausage and cheeses for their break-fast.

After glorious skiing all day, we would fall into bed for a be-fore-dinner rest. During one of these rests a bell started ringing. We were all out in the halls in a minute and the confusion among the hotel help was pure Italian. The bell ringing was tracked down to the room next to ours. There was a confused conclave in the hall and much shouting through the door. Somehow the wife in her bath had pressed something and started the bell ring-ing. I never knew what she did next, but the whole hotel was plunged into darkness. We had been a friendly group before, but after this experience, all barriers were down. At dinner that night there was that closeness that comes when people have shared an experience.

Kim and I usually went out to one of the hotels where there was dancing. One night, young George, a desperate George, asked me for help. He could go out sledding if he could find his bootlaces. Jerry had taken the laces because they were longer than his. Someone had tied them together so he could play with the kitten. When he and the kitten had tired, the laces had been dropped. We finally found them under a radiator. As we searched, I realized how intense the young can be. Kim and I walked over to the next hotel, our feet crunching in the crisp snow. There was a full moon, and we could see and hear George's happiness as he sped down the gentle slopes.

On New Year's Eve, something made us leave the dancing and go back to our hotel to welcome in the New Year. We were so glad we did. There were a few older Austrian couples and their faces lit up as we came in. At midnight we all sang and wished each other happiness. One of the gentlemen had little gifts for us all.

It was a grand holiday and, while we missed family, there was so much to do. There was not the desperate loneliness of the year before. We had enjoyed our friendship with the builder of bridges and his family. His wife was a maths teacher. Her great interest was in the pyramids of Egypt. Kim and I learned much from her.

As was our custom, we started home early, and it was good we did. By the time we reached Verona, we knew we were in for a bad fog. By the time we reached the exit for Brescia, we knew we could go no further. We inched our way along the streets of this city and finally found a hotel. It was a huge old place, so old that the light switch for our bedroom was on an outside wall in the hall. The bathrooms were out in the hall also, but we were so grateful to be out of the fog, we did not mind a bit. We found our way down to the vast dining room where one other guest was eating. Imagine our surprise when he turned out to be an Italian who spoke English fluently.

When we were ready for bed, it seemed very strange to step out into the hall to turn off the light. I suppose in olden days you rang for a servant to perform this service. We had our flashlight, which we blessed, for the room was huge. It was unbelievably quiet. The fog was so dense no one was out in the streets.

Next morning, the fog was still so bad we hesitated to drive. We made our way on foot to a number of interesting antiquities. We had everything to ourselves that day as no one else was about. The fog showed no sign of lifting, so after lunch we set off. It was easier in daylight, but we were thankful when we finally turned down our lane. Fritz gave us a friendly bark as we passed. How we blessed our oil heating when we opened our door and stepped out of the gray world. We soon had a fire crackling and our place became cozy, but it seemed strange without Mother.

However, now that we did not have Mother to consider, we could go skiing every weekend. On Thursday evenings, Kim would pack all our ski things in the car so he was all ready for his 7:30 departure for work. Mid-afternoon, in my ski clothes, I would catch the bus and go on around the lake to a little village near Kim's work. When he came along, we were off to a ski re-sort called Alpi di Mera. It was a picturesque drive through farmland and country villages. Children with pitchers would be going to the ever-flowing stream of water from the pipe in the village fountain. It was about supper time, so the men would be coming in from the fields.

We always had our supper in the same hotel restaurant right by the ski lift. The lift would be closed until 7:30, while the tow men dined. We almost always had mountain trout, as there was a fast-moving stream running past the hotel. The trout were de-licious. We and the other guests were in casual clothes, but the waiters were immaculate in their black tuxedos and white shirts. Like all the Italian waiters, we saw they moved about at a quick pace as though they really enjoyed their work.

The head waiter cut a very fine figure, and took his position very seriously. One evening he seemed sad and downcast. Kim whispered to me,"Let's give his spirits a lift. We'll order some-thing flambé." It worked like magic. As he got the flame going and things sizzling in his copper pan, he became a real maestro and whatever had been bothering him he forgot in the thrill of creating our dish.

After dinner we would get our things from the car and get on the ski lift. It was the kind where two people sat together side by side. A number of the seats would be filled with supplies for the six hotels up on the mountain top. That trip up could be intensely cold. After the first trip, I always brought newspaper to put over my legs. At the beginning of that long, slow ride, we looked down on earth and then snow. It was quiet, oh so quiet, and even when the moon was not full, you could feel the mystery of the woods. That time of suspension above the trees and the snow was a wonderful experience.

We tried three of the hotels on different weekends and settled on our favourite, which was farthest from the ski lift. The food was excellent. I always marveled at the elegant meals they could achieve with everything coming up on the lift. I loved the Italian sense of humour. One evening a young man said to the waitress,"No, no, no flowers tonight. I am not in a romantic mood."

Late Sunday afternoons, the wealthier would employ porters to carry their equipment and luggage to the tow. One porter was so heavily loaded he could barely walk. His fellow porters called out gaily,"Have a good holiday."

I had one hearty laugh on that mountain top. I do not know how many men were involved but, however many it was, they worked skillfully on their joke. As you drive along in Italy you frequently see the sign *"Lavoro in Corso,"* meaning "Work in Progress." Beautifully inscribed in the white snow beside one of the trails was *"Lavoro in Corso,"* and it was written in bright, yellow urine.

I have always treasured the American sense of humour, too. One big American working in Milan had come up for his first try at skiing. He made it very clear that the one expression he did not want to hear was "He died with his boots on."

He told us that he found he got better results in his business by employing Americans. The Italians he dealt with trusted Americans more than their own race. It was in the evenings after dinner when people sat around and talked that you learned things like this.

Later there was dancing to juke boxes. Once Kim and I went down to the dance room early and chanced on three young Italian children dancing. They were completely lost in the music as they twisted and gyrated.

Saturday mornings, I could cautiously join Kim on the bigger slopes, but by the afternoon and all day Sunday so many skiers came and skied so fast that I stayed on the easy slopes. One thing I could do was snowplow, and I helped many a beginner. Once I received a postcard from Milan expressing great thanks to me. Kim and I were at a complete loss to place the person and to think how I had been of service. Finally we remembered a young Italian engineer I had helped learn to snowplow.

Playing cards were expensive in Italy, so when we made our last trip I took up the three decks of cards that were given to us on shipboard at the Captain's party. The couple who owned our favourite hotel were so grateful that they gave us our wine for the entire weekend.

We treated ourselves to only one ski weekend in Switzerland. Bimbi and Reinier knew of a little place near St. Moritz. It was charming and the prices were low. We drove over to St. Moritz, skied there, saw the famous sleighs with the horses plumed and belled, and had one dinner in a very posh hotel. It was February and the skiing was so glorious, to give ourselves all of Sunday on the slopes, we decided to leave very early Monday morning. It was dark and quiet and, oh, so still up there in the mountains as we climbed into our cold car. We drove down, down through Switzerland and saw the stars dim and finally the sunrise light up the mountain tops. As we neared Lake Como in Italy, our breakfast time was drawing near. We realized we were coming to a market, for people with little wagons and on foot were going down the road. Many of the women were wearing an interesting type of straw hat with gay red ribbons. It was here that we saw one of the finest faces we had ever seen. It was a middle-aged woman swinging along and driving a brown goat to market. Her face was so arresting, Kim almost stopped the car. We would have loved a picture of her, but she had such character and dignity, a snapshot was out of the question.

As we breakfasted by the lake, the market procession passed us, and we were impressed by the distance some had travelled on foot. When we finally arrived at the marketplace, even though we were impatient to be on our way, there was nothing we could do. The stalls were so close on each side that we could have helped ourselves from the open car windows. We inched our way along, chuckling to think,"And this is the main and only road along this side of Lake Como." Luckily, we had left a good margin of time for travel so were able to enjoy the brown mountain faces about us.

There was much beaten copper in the stalls that I had not seen in any other markets. I can still see one plump, older man holding a pair of trousers up to himself, trying to judge the fit.

The time had come when Kim had short trips to make to Grenoble, Rome and Brussels. He would be away for a few days and we felt it was too expensive for me to go. When Mother was with us, Signora Bottini worried about the two of us down by the lake with no near neighbours, but when she realized I was going to be alone, she gave me no peace until I agreed to sleep at their villa. I wanted to be as little trouble as possible, so after dinner I would walk up the lane and then up the hill to their place. I would join the family in front of the television. Later we would retire, they to their side of the villa and their charming, forty-ish bachelor son and I to our side.

I deeply appreciated this arrangement, for I had perfect rest, whereas the one night I stayed alone down by the lake I was a bit apprehensive. There was only one problem. Gianmario and I shared the same bathroom, and I had never mastered how to completely flush those toilets with long chains and the reservoir up on the wall. I did not want him, an engineer, to think I was so careless as to leave the toilet unflushed. He was the type of man who never talked to me down by the roadside with his car motor running. Not only did he shut it off, but also got out of the car to talk with me. He had told me once that he was like butter in the sun when I sang. I just could not leave floating paper in the toilet for him to remember me by. After my first night of anguish, I solved my problem. I took a plastic bag inside a paper bag and made for my garbage pit before I climbed our outside stairway to get my breakfast.

A number of our Italian friends had small children and could not easily come out for dinner, since a babysitter had to be family. I made as typically Canadian meals as I could, wrapped them in blankets and took them to their homes. Stuffed pork tenderloin, canned corn (which I got in Lugano) and tomato aspic were favourites of my "meals on wheels."

The Bani's had two sons, Fulvio, aged five, and Stephano, aged seven, so I was able to invite them to the house. The usual Italian wife does not use her oven the way we do. I had baked and iced a layer cake, roasted a chicken and baked potatoes. The place looked cozy with our fire burning but I was a bit uneasy. Young children often do not adjust easily to different ways of cooking.

I waited a bit apprehensively, for once another Italian boy had whispered to his mother,"Do I have to eat this stuff?" Fulvio started to eat and said to his mother,"Could we come here to eat every night?" I could have hugged him.

He soon announced that he was hot as hell, and could he take his sweater off? Our place was much warmer than the high ceilinged, vast Italian rooms. None of them spoke English, and I was pleased I could follow so much of the conversation. The first time Stephano had ever seen a black man was on a train, and he had turned to his parents in amazement and said,"I thought we were travelling by day."

When Signor Bani tasted the cake, he said, "*Si vede che la Signora lavora con passione nella cuccina*" (It is evident that the Signora works with passion in the kitchen). When I make something Kim particularly approves of, I hear Signor Bani's words again.

One Sunday afternoon we set out with our map to find a place called Taino, as we had been invited there for tea at the villa of a man Kim had met at a trade mission in Milan. When we arrived in Taino, we asked for the villa Berini and were floored when we were told us there were many Berinis in Taino. Kim described our host, and some smiling women gave us his local nickname. Then the fun began, as we, obviously strangers in a French car, went along asking everyone we met for this man, using a very local pet name. His villa turned out to be well out of the town. On weekends, it contained three generations of the family, the oldest member, eighty-five, and the youngest, eighteen. The villa was very modern, most attractive and in great contrast to the buildings along the old winding streets of the ancient town.

During tea, I learned that Leonardo da Vinci had built a canal from Lago Maggiore. Not only is it still in use, but it was studied when the Panama canal was built. The two young men in the family had to leave early to get back to university. They, like their parents, spent every weekend with their grandparents, and I was impressed anew with the closeness of family ties. When it was our turn to leave, our host insisted on driving ahead to guide us through the maze of narrow streets. By now the town was like a fairy tale place with little candles twinkling everywhere, handsome gold and crimson banners and flowers cascading off the balconies. We had to wait for a procession decorated with more gold and crimson magnificence. It was all in honour of a priest who had been in Taino for forty years. Our host chuckled as he told us that many of the men walking along so devoutly in the procession were Communists.

The Bottini family always had a winter vacation on the Mediterranean Coast, and while they were away it was part of Giovanni's job to buy and take fresh flowers to the grave of their son. Ugo's father had died sixteen years ago and there were still fresh flowers on his grave every Sunday and a small vase of flowers by his photograph in the living room. The whole family gathered for mass on his birthday.

With family love so strong, I was interested in the attitude of the people towards religion. In our district, faith seemed more just a logical part of the daily routine and it was pretty well left to the women to attend church. When we did attend church on a Sunday in the city of Varese, there were many men in the congregation, and one had a tenor voice so sweet, so pure and beautiful that you could only think of choirs of angels.

On the whole, I would say the people did not have the feeling that religion was going to make them good, but rather would show them where they failed. In Italy *La Bella Figura*," the impression you make on others, is all important. Sad to say, *"La Figura del Prete,"* the figure cut by a priest, is not a compliment.

The country women associated themselves closely with the Virgin Mary. While city people told me the bands of black and white marble in churches were there because they were the colours of the wealthy Doria family, the country women told me they represented the joys and sorrows in the life of the Virgin. When I asked why they had their babies with no anesthetic, the reply was "The Virgin Mary had none." I know they felt it was better for the baby to enter the world without anesthetic. I often wondered if the poor ever felt there was too much wealth in the treasures of the church, but I never heard even a murmur of criticism.

Always in Italy there is the spell of the magnificence of the past. It was tangibly felt when the body of a beautiful young woman, wrapped in a golden shroud and adorned with jewels, was scooped out of the earth in Rome. Her handsome sarcophagus of pink marble was broken by a steam shovel excavating for a new building. This was on the northern outskirts of the city where the patricians had lived. She was so perfectly mummified that the police at first suspected a recent murder, but she had died eighteen hundred years ago.

I am sure every Italian spring is beautiful, but our last seemed heaven-kissed, and Kim and I were drinking deep. The apricot blossoms in Giovanni's orchard and then the peach blossoms up the tiered hillside behind the Bogni's villa had us lingering outside in the twilight. One morning, when I went up the lane for our milk, a cobweb in the fence was jewelled with dew and one apple blossom was caught in it.

We had arrived in May and were to leave in May. Kim's replacement, Stewart Russell, had arrived. His wife and two children would come when the school year was over. Through Angelo, we found a signora who spoke some English, and who was willing to take him as a boarder until his family arrived. Kim was introducing him to his work. I started in on the process of moving.

Our local friends, and a few from the Ispra Centre, bought all our furniture. It was quite unbelievable how fast it was spoken for. Soon all that was left was a gas heater I had bought for Mother (who loved heat the way Sam McGee did). I gave the heater to Giannina, as I knew her legs were often cold. Since we knew where everything was going, Kim and I made the most of April visiting favourite spots and taking countless pictures. It would be a special statue, the huge cedars of Lebanon and beautiful gates we loved.

There was one grief. Giannina and Signora Bottini did not want us to go, and every time they saw me, they said sadly "*cattiva, cattiva,*" meaning "naughty, naughty." I didn't want to leave them either, but it made it hard for me, as there was no way I could reason with them.

Italians have learned to accept so much that they can be very reasonable. Their attitude to stealing is as logical as this: "You leave things on the shore, and you know that when the waves come in, the things you have left will be carried away. If you leave things where they can be stolen, they will be." This they logically accept, but when it comes to partings they have no reason they can call on. Then, all is tears and sadness.

Kim and I loved Italy so much we wanted to leave something behind as a small "thank you." It was William Styron who said,"No one can possibly give more to Italy than he gets from it," and how right he was. We gave a maple tree to Italy. We had a planting ceremony in the grounds at Ispra. The Director, Dr. Kramers, and several colleagues, attended. A colleague from the Biology Department assured us it would thrive, even if he had to resort to intravenous feeding. It carries a tag, engraved in an alloy of zirconium, commemorating the cooperation of Canada with Euratom.

Even though we did not bring so much with us, I seemed to spend a fair amount of time packing. Every day or so another piece of furniture went to its new home. We finally ended up with our bed, six chairs, a table, an assortment of suitcases and some great woven baskets Kim could not resist.

Our grate fire added coziness to our emptying house and we always felt peace when one of the Calcinate fishermen slipped by in his crescent boat. I still treasure those last weeks, as Kim and I would sit after dinner and discuss our impressions and what we were going to miss. There would be no more girl garage attendants in smocks to beckon us out into the traffic. No more girls sitting sideways on the back of a Vespa with their ankles neatly crossed and their shoes not falling off (how they managed it, I never knew). We were going to miss the bargaining, the eyes of the seller filling with respect as he is beaten down. We would remember it as if it was a dueling match. "You are ruining me, but I admire your skill." We were going to miss our local *contadini* rythmically turning over the cut grass to dry. The grace of church steeples and red tiled roofs would stay with us.

We discussed surprises we had, like meeting Signor Bruno as he was coming back from a boar hunt on the borders of Hungary, in our early days, an Italian saying to Kim, "What shall we talk about – cars or women?". We were not prepared for the Italians' love of cars. We chuckled anew over a man we saw washing off his car, not with a pail, but with a silver champagne bucket. We remembered how at first the bureaucracy and procrastination nearly drove us mad, and how soon we were loving the Italians, their charm and their capacity to live and take pleasure in life. We agreed that they flatter you, but that you flower under it. It is a form of politeness and exerts you to do your best. My progress in Italian was proof of this.

We had soon realized that authority was weak, and that authority was resented and resisted. There was not the respect for law we know, as, for so many years, the laws were not made with their interests at heart. We had also learned that beneath the wild gestures and hot tempers, there could be cool reason and, in many, driving energy. Next to Germany, Italy had the most war damage. There was rubble and ruin, yet their trams and taxis were running when no one else had theirs in running order. They rebuilt and opened La Scala Opera House in one year. In the terrible flooding of November, 1966 industry was devastated, and by February of 1967, ninety percent had returned to full production.

I was so in love with Italians, I was ready to investigate any accusation against them. I had heard that they were poor fighters, and I checked with a number of soldiers of other nationalities. The verdict was: they can fight when they care about what they are fighting for. Then, their endurance is unbelievable.

The family is what they care about, and Kim and I found ourselves hoping, hoping that modern life would not erode the splendid solidarity of family life. When children live on love, not diversion, they grow up in a family tradition of good manners and dignity. I had noticed that children with Down's Syndrome looked more responsive and aware, and I wondered if it was due to the constant attention they received and the conversation that was always part of their lives.

Things we learned in Italy: to remember that "America" means South America. We had not known that, at peril to their lives, the Italians saved thousands of Jews. We realized again and again that in the past they had been kept ignorant by a minimum of schools and that they had been kept in want by persecution and capricious regulations, bewildered and insecure by arbitrary manipulation of vaguely worded laws. They had no clearly defined rights and duties; they were always granted favours. Because there were so many laws, ambiguous and contradictory, they would submit to injustice rather than go to all the trouble and expense of litigation. Because of poverty, ignorance and fear made them afraid of change, so they still clung strongly to tradition.

We realized Italians will lie to please, round off a picture, provoke an emotion. I found this lying to please maddening when I would be waiting for a bus and they told me it would be along shortly, when really it would be forty-five minutes. Somehow they felt my wait would be more pleasant if I expected it soon.

Our last guests at the lake were the Brodie family from Milan. He was the Canadian trade commissioner, opening a new Canadian mission in Milan. He and his wife and two daughters came for the day on a bright and beautiful Sunday in late April. We spent part of the time hunting for snails along the bank of the stream. Young Debbie was a keen student, and if she brought some snails, she would be granted a special privilege. As we scrambled and slipped along the bank of the stream, her father, Alex, confided to me that the special privilege was that she would be allowed to sing a song. I thought, if the whole class was as keen as she was, what a joy it must be to teach them.

That evening, as dusk fell, Debbie and her younger sister, Susie, saw their first fireflies. I would have loved a picture of the wonder in their eyes. The eyes of their mother, Joyce, really lit up when I offered her all the books in English that I had been able to acquire for Mother. It was real treasure.

When Alex found out our table and chairs were going to the Kramers' kitchen, he was sure he could get them onto the roof of his van. The children ran after fireflies as we roped the furniture on with my clotheslines. Europeans are not as free and easy as we Canadians, and many are quite position-conscious. Dr. Kramers is Dutch, and was the director of the laboratories at Ispra, but he never batted an eye as our Canadian Trade Comissioner from Milan drove up with his load of furniture.

Those chairs and that table have not left the lake of Varese. The Kramers loved Italy, as we do, and they have bought a holiday place across the lake from our little villa, and they tell us we are welcome to sit at our table again.

With the living room completely empty, the house really echoed. Kim had to go to Brussels and Grenoble. The Bottinis let us store our luggage in one of their bedrooms. Kim took off on his business trips and I went up to Switzerland to say goodbye to Alice and Karl, and our other dear friends Peter and Ruth. When we collected our belongings and fitted them into the car, the goodbyes were really sad and emotional. We spent our last night at the Albergo Europa, and had a last wonderful meal with the Stabilinis. Then we went out into the Piazza Monte Grappa for our last drink by the fountain.

Kim had to go to Rome and we decided to make Orvieto our overnight stop. We had always wanted to visit it to see its famous cathedral and because it produced Mother's favourite white wine. We drove quickly, but could still enjoy the beautiful spring. We could not take time to stop in Sienna, but drove slowly through, and vowed we would be back. There is a belief in Italy that Sienna was made invisible to the eyes of the enemy aviators by a miracle of the Queen of Heaven. There is no war destruction, so the spell of the past is not broken.

Before and after Sienna, we saw a number of signs advertising the Palace Hotel in Orvieto. What really interested us was that it had a garage. With our load of luggage, parking on the street did not appeal to us.

Orvieto is one of the hill-towns of the Roman plain. The grey of the stone was lovely, rising out of the lush green countryside. We were lucky enough to get into the garage, which turned out to be a cave in the rocky hillside just large enough for two cars.

This Palace Hotel had been a real palace and still had magnificent furniture and elaborate chandeliers. I could not imagine anyone settling down cozily with a book. One would have to live up to such elegance.

We will never forget walking down an ordinary street, not expecting anything, and there at the end of the street was the glory of the cathedral, its intricate mosaic façade lit by the setting sun. Glory is the right word, for this cathedral is one of the gems of Italy.

In Rome, we found a very pleasant small hotel near the Canadian Embassy, away from the centre of the city. It was convenient for Kim, as he had work to do at the Embassy. I made my way downtown by bus (proudly, I might say) and visited with Catherine and her children.

One day, I took the train south to have lunch and a last visit with our Israeli friends from the Poultry Exhibition. They were going back to Israel and were as sad to leave Italy as we were. On the trip down, the very friendly ticket taker spent quite a bit of time talking with me. I was proud of my Italian, but at a loss when he suggested we go off together for the afternoon. I said,"I am married." His logical reply was "But your husband is not here now."

Our parting was friendly, but I was relieved he was not on the return train. Jim Stone, our Senior Trade Commissioner, was throwing a party for our last evening in Rome. Our invitation said,"This is a party to say goodbye to yourselves." I came back to our hotel early to have a good rest before the party. When I asked for our room key I was given a note from Kim. "Don't go up to our room. Stew Russell was so desperate for sleep, he is bedded down in our bed." What to do that would be restful? I wandered the streets till I found a beauty salon, my first visit to one in Italy. Right away, I got into a struggle. Thank goodness my Italian was good enough to assure them I could not let them cut my hair as my husband liked it long. I came away with a marvelous, bouffant, Italian hair style. My hair had been teased and lacquered and was stiff as a helmet. Kim was enchanted with my new look.

It was a grand party. Chris and Jim had invited all our friends. Catherine and her oldest son were there, and surprised at my unexpected transformation since I had lunched with them.

The next morning, we set off early for Genoa, making Pisa our lunch stop. The sunshine was so brilliant and the Leaning Tower so dazzlingly white, we could hardly take the glare. It was thrilling to be right there and not straining to see as much as possible from a train window. We found a restaurant where we could eat in the shade under a trellis of grape vines. We asked the two men at the next table how long it would take us to get to Genoa. Quick as a wink came back "What kind of car do you drive?"

Sad to say, we arrived right in the midst of what seemed to be the busiest traffic time. Even sadder was that, in trying to see where Pina's street was, Kim went too close to the curb and cut a tire. I ran back a ways and placed our red triangle on the road to indicate "Beware – car trouble ahead." Then I stood on the curb with my heart in my mouth as Kim changed the tire while the traffic roared past.

When we finally arrived at Pina's door, we had to hold back our laughter as she fought her seven locks open, all the time talking away to us through the closed door. Once the door was open, what a welcome she gave us! Hers is a very loving heart and she has a special weakness for Kim. She helped him unpack, and there did not seem to be enough room in the huge walnut cupboard, so she just hung his suit coats on the corners of massive picture frames. Every picture in the room was at a rakish angle.

We had tried to get passage on a Norwegian freighter but had to settle for tourist class on the Christophoro Columbo. If we could have waited, we could have seen Charles again. He came in from Australia on the ship we would have sailed on. He went straight up to Varese, only to find we had left.

In those last days in Italy, Pina saw to it that we had all our favourite foods. She knew little restaurants where you got the best at the most reasonable prices. Her sister Anna and her niece did not speak English, and, when we spent Christmas of '51 in Genoa with Aunt Dorothy, we had no idea what interesting people they were. Then all we could do was exchange smiles. Now we could talk. As we sat after meals and talked, they were interested in sharing our impressions. How they laughed over my well-remembered terror that time in Varese, when the streets all filled with men and I thought some terrible national tragedy had befallen Italy. It was just that the men were having their eleven o'clock coffee break.

Pina has the greatest interest in other lands and their customs. She was delighted to hear that Kim found so many things in Italy that reminded him of China and that the two countries were alike in their close family life, their love of good food, ceremonies, feasts, elaborate rites and fireworks.

They were sorry we had missed seeing the apartment of the Court Dwarf at Mantua. It is sheer fantasy, even to a chapel. The dwarf was three feet tall, and his quarters were built in miniature. Whenever I think of Court Dwarfs, I wonder what it was like for the royal children to have someone their size with the wisdom of an adult.

They also told us that the black funeral launches in Venice are a sight to see, with gold swags, proud gold lions, palm fronds, red carnations and a black casket.

I had read in Jean Renoir's book, "Renoir, My Father," that the Italians had invented ceilings, parquet floors, locks, glass windows, chairs, forks, chimneys that drew properly, silks as fine as those from China, muslins, music, the theatre, opera... in short, almost every manifestation of social life.

We all agreed with this: we lovers of Italy. We were having such a happy time together it was hard to face our last day. Kim was so enamoured of my Italian hairstyle, he asked me please to have it done again. Our last morning, while he drove our car down to the ship, my hair was teased and lacquered once more. In the afternoon, when we went on board, Pina was standing on the pier to see us off. There was a young man standing near her, and Pina, who could never resist talking, was soon talking away earnestly to him. We knew she was telling him about us for he was soon straining to get a better look.

It was not really goodbye to Italy, for the ship was calling in at Naples, but when the ship's orchestra began "Arrivaderci Roma," I burst into tears.

I whispered to Kim *"Adesso una parte del mio cuore resterà sempre in Italia."* "Now a part of my heart will always remain in Italy."

To Italy, With Love

Chapter 12

Epilogue

I am back in Italy after an absence of ten years. In the months after Kate's death, I was overcome with the urge to return to the scenes of our sojourn on the Lake of Varese. I was also determined to reissue Kate's book, *Our Love Affair With Italy*, after careful editing and some rearrangement of chapters. I wanted to give her book a wider audience. To this end, I have brought her book with me to work on during my projected stay of three weeks in Italy.

The flight from Toronto with Alitalia was uneventful, though it left something to be desired in the way of service. When one is eighty-five and travelling business class, one might be forgiven for expecting a little coddling, but the expectation appears to be completely unreasonable in today's air travel. This trip has not been without the usual hassle both in Toronto and at Malpensa, Milan's international airport. I am coming to the conclusion that air travel is something that has to be endured, like a visit to the dentist. However, no luggage is lost and I arrive in one piece, for which I should be grateful, and I am.

When I last left Italy, after a visit in 1995, Malpensa was under construction. Ten years later, it is still under construction. This seems to be the fate of airports. My destination is a hotel/restaurant "Vecchia Riva" on the Lake of Varese at Schiranna, not far from where we used to live. I found Vecchia Riva on the Internet. It seemed ideally suited for my purpose.

Thankfully, I am met by Bepi at the airport. He is the youngest son of my good friend, Angelo. Angelo comes from an old Varese family and has three sons, each of whom has made his mark, and not only in Italy. Bepi, whom I can remember as a blond, blue-eyed child of eight, was twice a team member of Italy's entry into the Americas Cup yacht races. He is now a successful dentist in Varese. He is fifty-one years old, of medium height and slim, with a broad shouldered athletic build, his head still crowned with wavy blond hair, worn slightly long. He now has four sons of his own. The older of his two brothers, Claudio, has an international reputation as a successful yacht designer, and is the leader of the design team for Italy's current entry, "Luna Rossa," in the Americas Cup races in 2007.

Angelo can, of course, take a great deal of credit for these boys. He is a champion sailor himself and is a retired commodore of the local yacht club. But their success is in large measure due to their mother, Rina, who, completely undaunted by a household of four males, has devoted her considerable energies to keeping everyone looked after and in line. When Kate and I lived at the Lake, Angelo, Rina and the boys were frequent visitors. Angelo and Rina became friends for life.

My first impression on setting foot on Italian soil is that styles have changed. *"La bella figura"* is out and Grunge is in. One used to be surprised to find the silver-haired, well-dressed patrician with the slim briefcase to be no more than a minor clerk or salesman. Now shirts are made with short tails, meant to be worn outside the trousers. I was a little surprised to see Bepi's shirt-tail peeping out from under his sweater, but I shouldn't have been. Neckties are a thing of the past. Running shoes may be worn for any occasion, and the ubiquitous baseball cap is seen everywhere. As for women, anyone with a presentable midriff is showing it, more or less to advantage. The odd thing is that long, pointed shoes, that were very stylish in the mid 1950s, are now being worn everywhere, and the shop windows in Varese are full of them.

Another change is in the height of trees. Trees and children are faithful indicators of the passage of time, and in just ten years the growth of trees around the Lake of Varese is impressive. This is a region of rich, agricultural soil. Four and even five crops of hay may be taken off the land in a single season. On the drive from the airport, one gets the impression that trees are crowding in on both sides of the new highway from Malpensa to Varese.

If I had expected to be greeted with open arms at our destination, I would have been disappointed. Eight-thirty in the morning does not find the Vecchia Riva at its best. In spite of the international pretensions to be found on its website, it is in reality an Italian hotel meant for Italians. No one speaks English except Maureen, an attractive black waitress from Nigeria. The German spoken by Fiorenzo, the chief owner of the hotel, is atrocious.

Luciano, another of the owners (there are eight of them altogether) is said to be fluent in French but he is on holiday. I don't care. I love it. I love the location in tranquil surroundings about thirty metres from the shore of the Lake. My Italian is not half as good as I thought it was, but it is improving, and I can look forward to the food and the wine. The Vecchia Riva is only a couple of kilometres from Kate's and my villa on the lake, and therefore close to all the friends that we made during the years we lived there. I am looking forward to getting in touch with them.

The restaurant is the heart of Vecchia Riva; all else is secondary. My room is comfortable enough, furnished in the Spartan style of middle-class hotels in Italy. The walls are salmon pink, and there is a huge casement window opening onto the lake. The private bathroom is well appointed and spotless. There are no more than a dozen rooms in the hotel and there are few provisions for residents.

I discover, upon my arrival, that the restaurant is preparing for a sumptuous matrimonial celebration. Over one hundred family members and guests will be seated at lunch at one o'clock. Lunch will have many courses and will last for at least two hours, after which the party will pour out into the garden for high jinks and further refreshment while the luncheon tables are cleared and set up for the evening meal. This meal will go on into the small hours of the morning. There will be lots of noise. Italians love the sound of humanity. This is one thing that I expect has not changed.

I am not disappointed. I have collapsed on my bed about nine-thirty a.m. and have slept through to two in the afternoon. I am awakened by the sounds of celebration in the restaurant below. Maurizio, another of the owners, says I may have luncheon in the narrow *saletta* beside the bar. There I make the acquaintance of the father of the bride, a typical Varese businessman with a face like granite. He is paying plenty for this party.

The guests pour out into the garden, and from the door of the saletta I witness something I have never seen before. The friends of the groom have wrapped him up like a mummy in what appears to be duct tape, leaving only his head and feet exposed. They carry him around the garden like a log on their shoulders, face up, with a very suggestive flower thrust into the tape at his crotch. There is much shouting and singing. I am told later that friends of the groom are supposed to come up with some wild prank like this.

The sounds of voices goes on into the night. Even at one-thirty in the morning, I hear laughing and talking beneath my open window, the sound of children's voices mingled with those of men and women. I peep out of my casement window and see boys and girls of five and six running around under adult supervision. This is something in Italy that has not changed. Children are included in adult company at all times of the day and night. One result is that Italian children are seldom self-conscious in the presence of adults. On the other hand, as one Italian said to me some years ago, the trouble with Italians is that every child has been brought up with the firm belief that he or she is the centre of the universe.

Late at night, there is the sound of revelry farther down the lake. Judging from the distant chorus of young male voices, it may be a party held at the beginning of military service. The young men entering service collect money from their communities for a bang-up farewell party before donning the uniform. Considerable money was spent on fireworks in this case, for at twelve a.m. the lake reverberates to the explosion of thunder crackers, echoed and re-echoed by the surrounding hills.

I fall asleep, finally, at about two a.m. and sleep through what's left of the night. Next morning I am awakened by sounds of another kind. The Lake is gripped by one of the fiercest electrical storms I have ever experienced. Lightning and thunder are almost continuous. The noise, within the cup of surrounding hills, is deafening. Miraculously, there is no failure of electrical power. The whole demonstration is over in about five minutes, ending with a downpour of rain that is tropical in intensity.

Several days later, there is to be a second of these storms at eight-thirty on a Saturday morning. Fortunately, I am in my room when the rain starts, for it is accompanied by a driving west wind sweeping down the Lake, and I am just in time to close my shutters and my big casement window. Again, it is all over in a matter of a few minutes, but this time the power goes out. I am pleased to see that Vecchia Riva has emergency lighting in the hall and on the stairs. I time the outage: thirty-three minutes. Not bad under the circumstances.

In between these storms of tropical intensity are two or three days out of the Garden of Eden. The weather is sweet and there is not a cloud in the sky. In the morning, the chain of Alps to the north and west of us is clearly visible. Monte Rosa, the highest massif in these Alps, is brilliant in the morning sunlight, its snowy majesty seeming to float on a sea of clouds around its base.

This weather brings out the beauty of the Italian countryside. To someone coming from the New World, what is striking is that everything fits in. The houses, the trees and gardens, the fields and farms all seem to be arranged with exquisite taste. There is nothing that clashes, nothing ugly. This must be one of the qualities that has brought European visitors to Italy for centuries.

My friend Reinier, a Hollander, is one of the many Europeans who have chosen to live in this beautiful countryside. He has lived here for over forty years, has raised a family here, and has retired here. He lost his wife, Bimbi, in tragic circumstances, about four years ago. He speaks good Italian with a strong Dutch accent, and is outspoken in his criticism of Italy and Italians. Italians, he says, are in love with chaos and embrace it. That is why there are so many things here that don't make sense to other Europeans. To live in Italy, he says, one must do as the Italians do, or at least fit into the Italian way of life.

Angelo is one Italian who agrees with him. He is perpetually exclaiming and shaking his head over some aspect of Italian life. Yet, here he is at eighty-four, living very comfortably in Italy and enjoying it. He visited Vecchia Riva the other day and took part in an exercise that illustrates one aspect of Italian life, at once endearing and maddening. He was showing me where I can catch the bus going into the centre of the city of Varese. The bus stop was clear enough; it is the local terminus, about a hundred metres from the Vecchia Riva. Angelo was careful to explain that one must have a ticket, as the bus driver will not accept change, even though the ticket costs an even one Euro, and there is a one Euro coin. The terminus had no ticket vending machine. We were standing at the entrance to Varese's annual fair. Angelo thought that tickets could be bought at the fair office, and went in to inquire. They could not be bought there, but the general manager of the fair came back out with Angelo to engage in lively speculation as to where they might be bought. A tall and striking young woman passing by caught both the men's attention. They explained their problem to her. She was quite sure there would be a ticket outlet in the amusement centre in the adjacent park.

The amusement centre has a perfectly preserved, garishly coloured, vintage merry-go-round, and is run by a dear, elderly lady in bedroom slippers. She was sorry to tell us that one could not buy tickets in the amusement centre, but she was sure they could be bought at the terminus in Varese. This shifted the problem to another level. In the course of other inquiries, we did find out that the bus did not stop at the terminus where a large orange rectangle had been painted on the pavement, enclosing the word "BUS" in large letters, but at a temporary stop up the street. But there was still no answer to our problem. All of this took the better part of half an hour with no concrete result. I eventually discovered that tickets could be bought at the desk at Vecchia Riva, but one had to ask. I later discovered that many of the buses had ticket-dispensing machines on board.

The price of everything in Italy seems high to a visitor. Reinier says the reason is quite simple. If, when the Euro came in, it had been given a value corresponding to one of the European currencies, say, one Euro equals one Guilder, or one Deutschmark, or 1000 Lire, it would have been quite simple to relate prices in Euros to prices with which Europeans were familiar. But no, it was a matter of pride for the European Union to have a currency comparable to the U.S. dollar. This means that it is easy to lose sight of the intrinsic value of things when prices are expressed in Euros, a fact that opportunists in business do not fail to use to their advantage.

Angelo and his wife, Rina, are not lazy about calculating costs. Angelo keeps a running record of exchange rates and has a pretty good idea at all times of what he is paying. Reinier does the same thing. It is part of living in Italy.

I have timed my visit so as to have a couple of days with Reinier, who is leaving to visit his daughter in Idaho. His hair is completely white, but he, at least, has hair. Mine is merely a suggestion of hair. We have lunch at the Bel Sit for old times sake. The lunch is good, but expensive (it was on me). Bel Sit has been completely renovated, and is now a first-class hotel. Every room is beautifully decorated, equipped with a cordless laptop computer, and has a large, flat screen television. The view from windows on the second and third floor is enchanting, looking down the mountainside to the Lake of Varese, or west to Lake Maggiore and the Alps. One seems almost face-to-face with Monte Rosa at this elevation. The manager told me that the ballroom, where Kate and I used to dance, was still busy three times a week.

Reinier has put on a bit of weight, but not as much as I have. Angelo, on the other hand, has stayed trim and slim. The enormous mustaches he has affected since becoming commodore of the yacht club at Luino are streaked with grey, and his full head of hair is a uniform silver, but he shows no other signs of age. He has been struck, though, by a profound deafness. It is touching to see him straining to hear what one is saying. His wife, Rina, doesn't seem to age at all. Her hair is hardly touched with grey, and she seems as full of energy as ever. She prepared a wonderful lunch for our first reunion. I had by that time discovered where to get tickets for the bus, so bussed into Varese for the lunch, leaving my black fedora on the bus in my haste to get off.

I have now been here two weeks and have yet to see an obese Italian. These people eat enormously, yet manage for the most part to stay slim and trim. The food at the Vecchia Riva is excellent, and I have eaten a good deal of it, but if my waistband is any measure, I have not gained weight. (Note: This was wishful thinking. I have gained seven pounds.) Considering the prevailing problem of obesity in Canada, we surely have something to learn about the Italian diet. There may, of course, be other factors as well. For instance, it takes a lot of energy to talk like an Italian, and this may be a way of burning off fat, for Italians love to talk almost as much as they love to eat.

The cellphone was invented for Italians. Almost everyone has one and gives it good use. In Varese, I saw two young mothers side by side, wheeling their babies in carriages and each of the mothers was on a cellphone talking to somebody as they went along. Maria, Catherine's daughter, calling from Rome, says that cellphones are destroying the fabric of traditionally conservative Roman friendships. The constant chatter with anyone and everyone means that the hard won intimacy with close friends is a thing of the past.

As a guest at the Vecchia Riva, I have the choice on weekends of eating in the narrow *saletta* beside the bar, or going out to another restaurant. The dining room is always packed. During the week, I can sometimes eat in the dining room, for me a real pleasure. It is always entertaining to get there early and see a good restaurant come to life as the customers start to come in. Fiorenzo, the chief owner, and Mauro and perhaps Luciano, joint owners, are on duty, as are Maureen, Anna, Domenico and Lorenzo, who wait on table. Things start quietly, with owners and staff standing and talking in undertones. As business warms up, both owners and staff begin to move quickly and adroitly among the tables, using the small, quick steps of professionals, passing each other laden with plates of food, baskets of bread and flagons of wine and miraculously avoiding contact.

Fiorenzo, when he has his party seated, hovers over the table with his little notepad and recites what is available for the first and second plates of the meal. The first may be tagliatelli, stained black with the ink of squid, served with mussels and clams in their open shells, or a risotto with porcini mushrooms, or gniocci in a special Vecchia Riva sauce, or filets of lake perch on rice, or... it is a mystery to me how he remembers it all. The second plate may be a fillet of beef, a rack of lamb, a mixed grill (excellent) or chicken done in three or four different ways. How he keeps all the orders straight on his little pad is a further mystery, but everyone gets his or her order, and it comes piping hot, freshly cooked, from the kitchen.

If a guest so desires, he can begin by filling a plate from a huge selection of antipasto on sideboards near the entrance. Mauro and Luciano are doing the same thing at other tables, but, as the restaurant fills up, all three owners will pitch in with serving, clearing of plates and anything else that needs to be done. They have a gold mine in this restaurant, and they are working it for all that they are worth.

The Lake of Varese is important to the economy of the district, both as an essential source of water and as a scenic and recreational asset. It is tiny compared to its neighbours on either side, Lake Como or Lake Maggiore, but it has always played an important part in the history of the region. Situated just south of the city of Varese, it is nestled into the base of the mountain called Campo dei Fiori that dominates the city. Looking west to east, it is roughly the shape of a foot, nine kilometres from ankle to toe, and four wide between the arch and the heel. Kate and I lived on the lake midway along the arch between the hamlets of Gropello and Calcinate del Pesce. Even in those days, the lake was becoming polluted by discharge from the Ignis factory and from other municipalities around the lake. Thirty-three fishermen used to make a living fishing the lake, but the pollution gradually put an end to the fishing. Years ago, the fishermen launched a suit in Rome against Ignis for depriving them of their livelihood. According to Gianfranco, who lives just behind our old villa, the fishermen won their suit and the settlement was made two or three years ago. By that time, only three or four of the fishermen were still alive to reap their reward.

In recognition of the importance of the lake, local and provincial governments have made heroic efforts to clean up the water. Huge collector channels have been built along the north and south shores of the lake, collecting all the waste water discharged by the surrounding communities and carrying it to a treatment plant at the west end of the lake at a place called Bardello. Angelo and I have paid a visit to SOGEIVA, the society managing the treatment plant, and have been shown around by Paulo Bernini, the manager. In addition to treatment, the water is being aerated at different points in the lake to encourage natural bacterial action. The system has been up and running only since 2001, and data are still being collected, but the lake at Vecchia Riva is much cleaner than I remember it from forty years ago. Swimming is still prohibited, but this, too, may change.

Gianfranco is the son of Giovanni and Giannina, *contadini*, who farmed the land between our villa and the lakeshore road above. When Giovanni retired, he made the barn into a comfortable home, now owned by Gianfranco, himself retired since 2003, and his wife, Chiara. They have invited me to lunch and I have been admiring the handsome woodwork in the family room. Knowing that Gianfranco has worked in wood all his life, I ask if it is the handy work of Gianfranco, at which Chiara exclaims loudly that no, it is bought. Gianfranco will work for anyone but himself and Chiara. I have heard this complaint before in other families. The luncheon is delicious, a simple risotto with fresh mushrooms from the woods around us (where I used to find them), followed by medallions of pork tenderloin done in a cream sauce. There is a very passable local wine from the region (Bregano). Gianfranco says that there is a flourishing market for it over the border in France, for at 13.5% alcohol, it is much stronger than French wine. When the coffee is served, I am deeply touched to see that Gianfranco has bought a brand new bottle of grappa, because he knows that I like grappa in my coffee.

In conversation, I ask Gianfranco where he was when I telephoned to confirm the luncheon engagement. "I was out cutting the grass," he says. "Oh, using the *ranza*, I suppose," I say. "*La ranza*" is local dialect for the slim, razor-sharp scythes of the region. "Oh no, nobody uses the *ranza* any more. I used the lawn-mower." He and his family have five cars parked in the fore-yard.

I am coming to the end of my stay in Italy when I receive a visit at the Vecchia Riva that is the crowning pleasure of my stay. I have been here three weeks and have established contacts and renewed many friendships, particularly those in Calcinate near our home on the lake. Giovanna was a beautiful child of eight when we lived in Italy. Serious and intelligent, she was always at the head of her class at the school in Calcinate; but she would break into a radiant smile at the slightest hint of fun. We have made telephone contact early in my visit. Yes, she is the grand-daughter of Signora Zanetti. Yes, she is the daughter of Carmelina. Yes, she grew up in Calcinate. Yes, she remembers well the *signori canadesi* who lived on the lake. All this with in-creasing excitement on both ends of the line. She is married and has a daughter of her own, has her own business as a project planner and controller, and maintains an office near her home in Calcinate. She has kept her maiden surname because of her pro-fessional contacts. She and her husband must leave almost im-mediately on a tour of Egypt, her first real holiday in years, but she will be back before I leave.

Angelo has taken me in Bepi's Land Rover to visit Giovanna's mother, Carmelina, and her aunt, Piera, in their homes in Calcinate. They are the daughters of Kate's special friend, Signora Maria Zanetti. We knew from previous visits that both sisters had been widowed. It is a joyful reunion, and I realize anew what wonderful friends they were to us, strangers and for-eigners that we were, when we lived on the lake.

Giovanna's daughter, Marta, has made an appearance, and I am struck by how much like Giovanna she is. "Well," says Marta matter of factly,"she is my mother and I am her daughter." Marta is twenty-two and teaches school. She takes us to the splendid villa, a little up the hill, in which she lives with her grandmother, her mother, and her father. Her Aunt Piera has kept her traditional Calcinate residence, but has given up the upper floor to Giovanna's office.

Now Giovanna is back from Egypt, and here she is. She has come by herself to Vecchia Riva, and has recognized me at a distance, sitting in the garden of the hotel. I recognize her the moment I look into those intelligent brown eyes. She is fifty-one now and still beautiful, slim, petite and elegant. But she is a person of importance, and is accustomed to making decisions and giving directions. Still, it is lovely to see that radiant smile now and then as we remember old times. We will keep this friendship going as long as we can.

Giovanna's visit leaves me in a happy daze. I am to leave next morning, but I am already planning for the next trip. Will I come back to Vecchia Riva? I don't know, but Fiorenzo, Mauro, Luciano, Maurizio and the others are now my friends. And of course the food is wonderful. I guess maybe I'll be back.

Angelo and Rina have come to say their farewells. Angelo comes around the corner of the Vecchia Riva waving my black hat on the end of my cane, which I had left somewhere. He has been diligent at the lost-and-found department of the bus company. That is something else that has changed in Italy. When Kate and I were living at the lake we would have kissed that hat and cane goodbye.

This visit has been a success in every respect. I have "held court" at the Vecchia Riva for the past three weeks, during which friends have come from all over to visit and renew friendships: Catherine's children, our friends Karl and Alice from Switzerland, our friends from Varese, Calcinate and from Ispra, and others who have telephoned from Rome and Pescara. It has been an epiphany of friendship, inspired, in the first instance, by Kate. Giovanna put it best when she said that, even as a child, in awe of the strange *signori canadesi*, she responded immediately to the sympathy and affection that were so much a part of Kate.

POSTSCRIPTUM

This story would not be complete without reference to Kate's special friend, Bruna. I did not make contact with her on my visit to Italy, but have since found her through the good offices of her daughter, Celestina, who still lives in Calcinate. Bruna is eighty-three and lives alone in Padova not far from her other daughter, Maria Louisa. When I telephoned her from Canada and told her who I was, she shrieked with joy. My Calcinate friends still use the respectful form of Italian with me, but not Bruna. She enfolded me at once into the intimate form of address. She had fallen and broken her two front teeth, so her speech was lisping; but there was no doubt about her sincerity. She has since had the teeth repaired (at a cost of four million lire, she says. No euros for Bruna!) and we communicate regularly by telephone on Sundays. I call my other Italian friends, too. The calls have all been from Canada to Italy, but it has been not so with Bruna. She surprises me, to her great delight, by calling me on occasion. She writes, as well. She recently read to me a poem on growing old that she had composed. I was impressed. One always feels with Bruna that one is dealing with someone to be reckoned with. Kate's loving and respectful judgment of Bruna was unerring, as usual.